# MODERN ROBOTICS

## BUILDING VERSATILE MACHINES

Harry Henderson

**CHELSEA HOUSE**
PUBLISHERS

An imprint of Infobase Publishing

To the researchers who are finding in robots
a mirror in which to learn more about humanity.

**MODERN ROBOTICS: Building Versatile Machines**
Copyright © 2006 by Harry Henderson

Chelsea House
An imprint of Infobase Publishing
132 West 31st Street
New York NY 10001

**Library of Congress Cataloging-in-Publication Data**

Henderson, Harry, 1951–
    Modern robotics: building versatile machines / Harry Henderson.
        p. cm. — (Milestones in discovery and invention)
    Includes index.
    ISBN 0-8160-5745-1
    1. Robotics. I. Title. II. Series.
    TJ211.H36 2006
    629.8'92—dc22                              2005031805

Chelsea House books are available at special discounts when purchased in bulk
quantities for businesses, associations, institutions, or sales promotions. Please call
our Special Sales Department in New York at (212) 967-8800 or (800) 322-8755.

You can find Chelsea House on the World Wide Web at
http://www.chelseahouse.com

Text design by James Scotto-Lavino
Cover design by Dorothy M. Preston
Illustrations by Sholto Ainslie and Melissa Ericksen

Printed in the United States of America
MP FOF 10 9 8 7 6 5 4 3 2 1

This book is printed on acid-free paper.

# CONTENTS

# PREFACE

The Milestones in Science and Discovery set is based on a simple but powerful idea—that science and technology are not separate from people's daily lives. Rather, they are part of seeking to understand and reshape the world, an activity that virtually defines being human.

More than a million years ago, the ancestors of modern humans began to shape stones into tools that helped them compete with the specialized predators around them. Starting about 35,000 years ago, the modern type of human, *Homo sapiens,* also created elaborate cave paintings and finely crafted art objects, showing that technology had been joined with imagination and language to compose a new and vibrant world of culture. Humans were not only shaping their world but representing it in art and thinking about its nature and meaning.

Technology is a basic part of that culture. The mythologies of many peoples include a trickster figure, who upsets the settled order of things and brings forth new creative and destructive possibilities. In many myths, for instance, a trickster such as the Native Americans' Coyote or Raven steals fire from the gods and gives it to human beings. All technology, whether it harnesses fire, electricity, or the energy locked in the heart of atoms or genes, partakes of the double-edged gift of the trickster, providing power to both hurt and heal.

An inventor of technology is often inspired by the discoveries of scientists. Science as we know it today is younger than technology, dating back about 500 years to a period called the Renaissance. During the Renaissance, artists and thinkers began to explore nature systematically, and the first modern scientists, such as Leonardo da Vinci (1452–1519) and Galileo Galilei (1564–1642), used instruments and experiments to develop and test ideas about how objects in the universe behaved. A succession of revolutions followed, often introduced by individual geniuses: Isaac Newton (1643–1727) in mechanics and mathematics, Charles Darwin (1809–1882) in biological evolution, Albert Einstein (1879–1955) in relativity and quantum physics, James Watson (1928–   ) and Francis Crick (1916–2004) in modern genetics. Today's emerging fields of science and technology, such as genetic engineering, nanotechnology, and artificial intelligence, have their own inspiring leaders.

The fact that particular names such as Newton, Darwin, and Einstein can be so easily associated with these revolutions suggests the importance of the individual in modern science and technology. Each book in this set thus focuses on the lives and achievements of eight to 10 individuals who together have revolutionized an aspect of science or technology. Each book presents a different field: marine science, genetics, astronomy and space science, forensic science, communications technology, robotics, artificial intelligence, and mathematical simulation. Although early pioneers are included where appropriate, the emphasis is generally on researchers who worked in the 20th century or are still working today.

The biographies in each volume are placed in an order that reflects the flow of the individuals' major achievements, but these life stories are often intertwined. The achievements of particular men and women cannot be understood without some knowledge of the times they lived in, the people they worked with, and developments that preceded their research. Newton famously remarked, "If I have seen further [than others], it is by standing on the shoulders of giants." Each scientist or inventor builds upon—or wrestles with—the work that has come before. Individual scientists and inventors also interact with others in their own laboratories and elsewhere, sometimes even partaking in vast collective efforts, such as the government and private projects that raced at the end of the 20th century to complete the description of the human genome. Scientists and inventors affect, and are affected by, economic, political, and social forces as well. The relationship between scientific and technical creativity and developments in social institutions is another important facet of this series.

A number of additional features provide further context for the biographies in these books. Each chapter includes a chronology and suggestions for further reading. In addition, a glossary and a general bibliography (including organizations and Web resources) appear at the end of each book. Several types of sidebars are also used in the text to explore particular aspects of the profiled scientists' and inventors' work:

**Connections** Describes the relationship between the featured work and other scientific or technical developments.

**I Was There** Presents first-hand accounts of discoveries or inventions.

**Issues** Discusses scientific or ethical issues raised by the discovery or invention.

**Other Scientists (or Inventors)** Describes other individuals who played an important part in the work being discussed.

**Parallels** Shows parallel or related discoveries.

**Social Impact** Suggests how the discovery or invention affects or might affect society and daily life.

**Solving Problems** Explains how a scientist or inventor dealt with a particular technical problem or challenge.

**Trends** Presents data or statistics showing how developments in a field changed over time.

Our hope is that readers will be intrigued and inspired by these stories of the human quest for understanding, exploration, and innovation. We have tried to provide the context and tools to enable readers to forge their own connections and to further pursue their fields of interest.

# ACKNOWLEDGMENTS

I would like to express my gratitude to robotics researchers Joseph Engelberger, Rodney Brooks, Marc Raibert, and Donna Shirley for taking the time from their busy schedules to answer questions and provide feedback and photographs. I would also like to thank the folks at Honda Motor Corporation and iRobot, Inc. for their help in obtaining information and photographs. My editor, Frank Darmstadt, deserves special thanks for his patient help seeing this project through to its conclusion. And also a special thanks to copy editor Amy L. Conver. Finally, I am thankful every day for sharing my life with my wife, Lisa Yount: fellow author, burgeoning artist, and always best friend.

# INTRODUCTION

Although true robots are a creation of the second half of the 20th century, the *idea* of the robot has stirred the human imagination for a much longer period of time.

Images of artificial people and mechanical servants stretch back even to the days of ancient myth. For example, the Greek god of metalwork, called Vulcan or Hephaestus, was said to have created two kinds of mechanical servants: graceful golden handmaidens and (more practically perhaps) tables that walked by themselves on three legs.

In medieval Jewish lore, a golem was a clay statue that could be animated by a magician using incantations from the Kabbalah. The instructions for a golem's operation were inscribed on a scroll and placed inside the being's head. In one legend, a golem was given instructions to fill a well, but its scroll did not tell it when to stop filling it. Soon the house was overflowing with water in what was perhaps the world's first programming error. Fear of losing control has always been part of our primal response to robots.

## Automatons and the Age of Reason

The Renaissance brought new interest in the structures and mechanisms of the human body, and in the late 15th and early 16th centuries, the famed artist-inventor Leonardo da Vinci made sketches of many mechanisms based on principles he found in nature. One such drawing showed a mechanical knight that could move its head and jaw, sit up, and wave its arms.

By the 18th century, the construction of elaborate automatons had become the rage in the royal courts of Europe. One inventor,

Jacques de Vaucanson, built an android or humanlike automaton that could play the flute. Another Vaucanson creation, a mechanical duck, could simulate eating, digestion, and defecation. It should be noted, however, that these automata, despite their complexity, were not true robots in the modern sense. Everything they did was dictated step by step by the action of clockwork, cams, or other mechanisms. Their actions were fixed and unvarying, without regard for the people or things in the surrounding environment.

The automaton seemed to symbolize the triumph of the Age of Reason, a time when a newly confident science mastered the secrets of gravity and motion. To many observers, these developments in theory and technology suggested that if a machine could be made to imitate the actions of animals and even people, perhaps living things were merely elaborate automatons whose mechanism would soon be uncovered by science.

# Anticipating Robots: 20th-Century Science Fiction

At the dawn of the 20th century, an explosion of new scientific theories and inventions led to the creation of a literature that sought to explore their implications and a variety of possible futures. In the science fiction magazines of the 1920s and 1930s, the alien "bug-eyed monsters" were often accompanied by hulking robots. These robots were often relentless in their attempts to carry out some sort of evil plan.

Robots also appeared in other media. Indeed, the word *robot* is first found in the 1921 play *Rossum's Universal Robots* by the Czech playwright Karel Capek. Here and in Fritz Lang's 1927 movie *Metropolis,* the robot took on a social dimension, symbolizing the threat of automation to human livelihoods and suggesting the relentless metronome-like pace of the industrial world.

While many writers caused people to fear robots, Isaac Asimov inspired a generation of engineers to *build* them. In Asimov's stories, robots were the (usually) reliable servants of humankind, built to obey laws that would prevent them from harming people.

## Robots' First Steps

The development of the digital computer as well as sophisticated electronics and control systems during the 1940s gave engineers the practical means to start building real robots. This book's first featured scientist, Norbert Wiener, a mathematician whose interests ranged from computers to game theory to neurology, provided in cybernetics a badly needed theoretical framework for understanding communication, feedback, and control in machines—including robots.

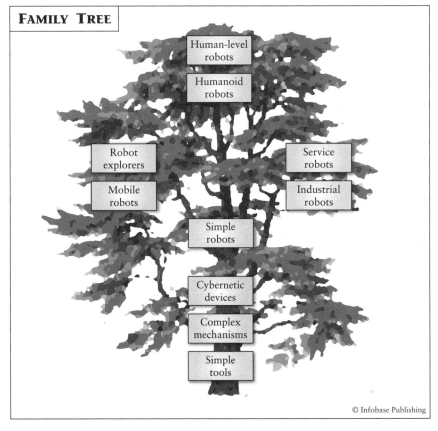

**FAMILY TREE**

Human-level robots

Humanoid robots

Robot explorers

Service robots

Mobile robots

Industrial robots

Simple robots

Cybernetic devices

Complex mechanisms

Simple tools

© Infobase Publishing

*A family tree shows how robots developed from increasingly complex tools and machines. After they gained mobility, robots then branched into a variety of roles, with the potential of becoming humanlike in structure and behavior.*

Researchers such as Grey Walter began to build robots that rolled about on their own, searching for light sources or otherwise interacting with the environment. By the mid-1960s, a rather wobbly robot called Shakey was slowly navigating its way down the corridors of the Stanford Research Institute, attempting to interpret pictures taken through its television camera.

The first real impact of robots, however, came when engineer-entrepreneur Joseph Engelberger and inventor George Devol created Unimate, the first industrial robot, which went to work in a General Motors plant in 1961. Unimate was essentially a big arm that could be fitted with various kinds of grasping devices and tools. Precisely positioned, the robot could work tirelessly at jobs that were either dangerous or unpleasant for human workers (such as casting and handling red-hot car parts) or were tedious but required consistent precision (such as riveting or painting).

Industrial robots increased productivity and helped factories remain competitive. The Japanese in particular embraced robots in the 1970s. Although some people feared that the industrial robot would lead to a massive loss of jobs for human workers, this first wave of robots did not cause much disruption.

## Mobile Robots and Explorers

Industrial robots were fixed to the assembly line. Robotics researchers were also learning how to create robots that could move freely in the environment, perceiving and reacting to humans and their world. Starting in the 1970s, considerable strides were made in developing navigation systems for robots. By the end of the decade, Hans Moravec had improved the Stanford Cart, one of the first autonomously navigating robots, so that it could (slowly) find its way through a room strewed with chairs without bumping into any.

By the 1980s, robots were even learning to walk like people and other animals. Marc Raibert's "Leg Laboratory" at the Massachusetts Institute of Technology (MIT) analyzed the gaits of humans and animals and created robots that could walk on two or four feet or even hop like kangaroos. Other researchers such as

Rodney Brooks (also at MIT) looked to insects as their inspiration for walking robots.

The coming of the Space Age and the desire to explore the solar system beyond the reach of human astronauts led to the development of robot space probes. At MIT and the Jet Propulsion Laboratory in Pasadena, California, researchers developed robots that could travel millions of miles to gather data from Mars and other planets. Viking landers sampled the soil of Mars in 1976. By the end of the century, thanks to the work of robotics researchers and engineer-managers such as Donna Shirley, mobile robots had become planetary rovers that could drive around Mars looking for interesting rocks and formations.

## From Helpers to Companions

Back on Earth, mobile robots have started to become useful in everyday life. In some hospitals, HelpMate robots (developed by the same Joseph Engelberger of Unimate fame) can be found delivering medicine and records without human supervision. Robots are even starting to become household appliances. The robot vacuum cleaner Roomba (created by Colin Angle, Helen Greiner, and Rodney Brooks) can do a decent job of keeping the floor clean. Tomorrow robots may help the elderly get around, fetch things for them, and monitor their medical condition.

The ultimate robots—the ones first seen in myth and later in science fiction—are the ones that look and act like people. Honda's Asimo robot (developed by a team led by Hirose Masato) looks like a tall child and walks and jogs sure-footedly. But the essence of humanoid robots also includes the possibility that they might think, learn, and even feel the way we do. Rodney Brooks's and Cynthia Breazeal's work during the 1990s with the robots Cog and Kismet expressed a much more organic approach to robot development. These robots generated their actions out of the complex interaction of sense perceptions, movement, and the cues they observed in the humans around them. The hope of these researchers is that robots can become social beings.

Serious robotics research inevitably brings one to basic philosophical questions. As robots become more sophisticated, they become mirrors in which we see something similar to ourselves in some ways yet alien in others. Researchers draw different conclusions about how robots may challenge or transform us. Hans Moravec believes that robots will reach and then surpass human intelligence around the middle of this century. Kevin Warwick, creator of the first human neural implant, believes that as robots become more like us, we should become more like them—"cyborgs" who can use robotic technology to extend the capabilities of the human body and mind.

What will the future interactions of people and robots be like? Rodney Brooks sounded a hopeful note on the BBC news program *Hardtalk* on August 19, 2002: "Every technology, every science that tells us more about ourselves is scary at the time. We've so far managed to transcend all of that and come to a better understanding of ourselves."

On a practical level, this understanding is creating a new hybrid science of biology and robotics. Mitsuo Kawato, director of the ATR Computational Neuroscience Laboratories in Kyoto, Japan, explained new developments in the January 2005 issue of MIT's *Technology Review*. Kawato's laboratory is using detailed scans of human brains to help design a robot that has neural and brain structures similar to those of a human child. Kawato explained that "Only when we try to reproduce brain functions in artificial machines can we understand the information processing of the brain."

# 1

# A NEW SCIENCE

## NORBERT WIENER AND CYBERNETICS

By the 20th century, people had developed many sophisticated devices, ranging from steam engines and elaborate manufacturing equipment to intricate telegraph and telephone networks. The more complicated the machine, the harder it is to control. As a result, there was an increasing effort to create automatic control-and-switching systems that could prevent freight trains from colliding or route telephone calls across hundreds of miles. Further, the challenges of 20th-century warfare would bring the need for systems that could, for example, allow antiaircraft guns to track and predict a bomber's path.

Only electronic circuits that could react at the speed of light would prove to be fast enough to respond to these challenges. But even as engineers created new electronics applications, scientists found they were lacking a comprehensive theory that could explain how signals—information—flowed between machines and their environment. Without such a theory, engineers were finding that controls were not behaving as expected—for example, an automatic antiaircraft gun would often slew back and forth rather than locking on to the target plane.

Gaining a true understanding of communications and control systems would require contributions from biology (particularly neurophysiology), new forms of mathematics, and the emerging field of digital computing design. One mathematician, Norbert Wiener, would draw insights from these and other fields together, creating a new science that he would call cybernetics. In turn,

1

*Norbert Wiener contributed to many fields of mathematics and science, but his development of cybernetics, the science of communication and control, provided fundamental principles for the design of complex machines such as robots.* (©American Institute of Physics, Emilio Segré Archive)

cybernetics would form a crucial theoretical basis for modern robotics and automation.

## Child Prodigy

Norbert Wiener was born on November 26, 1894. His father was a teacher of modern languages at the University of Missouri, and his mother was also well educated and cultured. Wiener's parents recognized quickly that he was an exceptional child. Wiener learned the alphabet when he was only 18 months old. When he was little more than a toddler, Wiener loved to sit under the desk in his father's study and read books he had selected for their interesting pictures and words that he could puzzle out. Illustrated science books and magazines were his favorites—particularly natural history.

Surprisingly, young Wiener's math skills fell short of his literary attainments. Wiener's father decided to intervene in his son's education. Under this attention, the boy progressed rapidly in math and other fields, but it was not without cost. In the first volume of his autobiography, *Ex-Prodigy*, published in 1953, Norbert Wiener recalled typical algebra sessions with his father:

> *Every mistake had to be corrected as it was made. He would begin the discussion in an easy, conversational tone. This lasted exactly until I made the first mathematical mistake. Then the gentle and loving father was replaced by the avenger of the blood. The first warning he gave me of my unconscious delinquency was a very sharp and aspirated "What!" and if I did not follow this by coming to heel at once, he would admonish me, "Now do this again!" By this time I was weeping and terrified.*

Words of praise were few and far between, while shame and humiliation were often prolonged. In his autobiography, Wiener would express great respect for his father, but he would also recount the psychological pain involved in their relationship. Throughout his life, Wiener would also suffer from what is today called bipolar disorder, characterized by steep mood swings.

Unlike some child prodigies, young Wiener was energetic and enjoyed physical activity such as hiking and exploring the countryside, as well as taking part in farm chores. Unfortunately, the boy was physically clumsy, in part because of his poor eyesight. As Wiener later observed in his first autobiography:

> *Muscular dexterity . . . depends on the whole chain which starts in the eye, goes through the muscular action, and there continues in the scanning by the eye of the results of this muscular action. It is not only necessary for the muscular arc and the visual arc to be perfect, each by itself, but it is equally necessary that the relations between the two be precise and constant.*

In his second autobiographical volume, *I Am a Mathematician*, published in 1956, Wiener elevated walking to a metaphor about the precariousness of life:

> *The equilibrium of the human body, like most equilibria which we find in life processes, is not static but results from a continuous interplay of processes which resist in an active way any tendency for them to lead to a breakdown. Our standing and our walking are thus a continual jujitsu against gravity, as life is a perpetual wrestling match with death.*

Perhaps it was because Wiener could not take natural coordination for granted that he would be driven to study it in such detail and create new science to explain it.

Wiener was eventually returned to the school system, graduating from high school when he was only 11 years old. A year later, Wiener enrolled at Tufts College (later Tufts University) in Medford, Massachusetts, and he was featured on the pages of the *New York World* as the youngest college student in American history. Wiener wanted to major in zoology, but as he noted later in his autobiography, his chemistry classes resulted in "probably the greatest cost in apparatus per experiment ever run up by a Tufts undergraduate"—and the results of dissections in the biology lab were little better. Gradually, these physical failures drove him to focus more on mathematics, where "one's blunders . . . can be corrected . . . with a stroke of the pencil." After only three years, the now 15-year-old Wiener earned a bachelor's degree in mathematics. By then mathematics professors were even letting him lecture to their classes.

## Brilliant Mathematician

Enrolling at Harvard, Wiener made another attempt to study zoology, but he proved to be as uncomfortable as ever with laboratory work. Partly at his father's urging, he then accepted a graduate scholarship at Cornell University, where he studied philosophy and mathematics. Still dissatisfied, Wiener returned to Harvard in 1911, where he was able to pursue the philosophy of mathematics. He obtained his master's degree in 1912, with the Ph.D. following only a year later. Wiener's doctoral dissertation was on mathematical logic (rules for proving assertions). At this time, this was a "leading edge" topic in which mathematicians were struggling to define the limits of their field.

Along with his doctorate, Wiener had earned a fellowship that allowed him to study with some of Europe's most prominent mathematicians. These included British mathematician-philosophers Bertrand Russell and Alfred North Whitehead (who had coauthored a book called *Principia Mathematica* that defined modern mathematics), G. H. Hardy, as well as leading German figures such as David Hilbert. After his return to the United States in 1915, Wiener took various instructorships.

As the United States began to edge toward entering the world war that had broken out in Europe in 1914, Wiener joined the staff at the Proving Ground at Aberdeen, Maryland. He became involved in the effort to find faster ways to calculate the tables needed for aiming the increasingly rapid-firing artillery that was coming into use.

## Life at MIT

After the war, Wiener obtained a teaching position at the Massachusetts Institute of Technology (MIT), where he would spend the rest of his career. At the time Wiener arrived, mathematics was only a secondary concern at that institution, which was principally an engineering school. Wiener's strong interest in the mathematical explanation of physical processes meshed well with MIT professors who were concerned about the institute's lack of theoretical rigor and the need for mathematical sophistication to match the complexity of the new electronic devices researchers were creating.

During the 1920s, Wiener would make important contributions to the study of Brownian motion (the seemingly random, continuous movement of molecules) as well as harmonic analysis. The latter involves the breaking down of complex waveforms (such as in electronic signals) into manageable components.

In 1933, Wiener met Arturo Rosenblueth, a Mexican neurophysiologist who had started a wide-ranging informal seminar that brought together biological and physical sciences. Wiener was drawn to it not only from his lifelong interest in natural history but also by the challenge to apply mathematical ideas and communications theory to biology, a field that had seen little mathematical analysis. Wiener began to think about the similarities between electronic circuits and the nervous systems of animals.

Meanwhile, Wiener had also worked with Vannevar Bush, another versatile mathematician and systems thinker who had developed a complex analog computer that could solve equations with many variables. (An analog computer uses physical forces such as electricity to model and solve equations.) In beginning to think about the structure of computing machines, Wiener joined other researchers who would soon be launching a revolution in information processing.

## Stopping the Bombers

In 1939, Europe again plunged into war. Weiner, who had not learned much about his Jewish ancestry until later in life, worked hard to help German Jewish scientists who had become refugees in America. As it became clearer that the United States would enter World War II, Wiener also returned to the problem of ballistics, or the analysis of trajectories of flying objects.

Bomber planes could now fly much higher and faster than the early machines of the previous war. This in turn meant that tracking planes and aiming antiaircraft guns by hand would no longer be sufficient. This was particularly true because bomber pilots would be maneuvering to throw off the gunners' aim. Nevertheless, Wiener was able to apply the statistical analysis that had enabled him to work with the random Brownian motion of molecules to dealing with the gun-aiming problem. He realized that while the evasive maneuvers might be somewhat random, they were limited by the physical characteristics of both plane and pilot. For example, a plane can only turn or dive so fast without having its wings come off or the pilot "black out." Applying appropriate "statistical constraints,"

## I WAS THERE: "WIENER WALKS"

Fellow faculty members and students at MIT found Norbert Wiener to be an intriguing, baffling, and sometimes infuriating "human phenomenon." In their biography of Wiener, Flo Conway and Jim Siegelman described what became known as "Wiener Walks":

> *[Wiener] was a man in near perpetual motion. Inquisitive, gregarious, garrulous. Wiener made a habit of walking MIT's maze inside and out. By the mid-1930s, the entire campus had adapted to the daily spectacle of the bespectacled Wiener waddling along the university's byways and beaten paths, waving an ever-present cigar, expounding in his booming voice on the most near and far-fetched topics . . .*

Many amusing Wiener stories became part of campus lore. One time Wiener apparently went into the wrong classroom and delivered a lecture to the bemused students. Another time Wiener entered a class (one of his own, this time), strode up to the blackboard, wrote a "4," and walked out. Only later did the students realize that Wiener had indicated that he would be away for four weeks' vacation.

There was usually a method to Wiener's waywardness, though. Conway and Siegelman quoted one student describing his encounter with Wiener:

> *He stopped me halfway, we happened to be going in opposite directions, and he raised some question he wanted to discuss. When we finished talking, he started to walk away and then he turned around suddenly, came back and asked, "By the way, which way was I headed before we met?" I said, "You were going toward Building 8." And he said, "Thanks, that means I've already had my lunch."*

Wiener could be rude and inconsiderate. He fell asleep easily (he suffered from apnea, a condition where breathing is disrupted and sleep interrupted). Yet Wiener could snore away quite loudly during a lecture but then wake up and make a comment that seemed perfectly relevant.

Wiener was able to create a prototype gun-aiming device that could predict a target plane's location with enough accuracy to improve considerably the chances of shooting it down.

## Feedback

The ballistics work would help Wiener develop a key concept, feedback. As the plane moved, the tracking device had to readjust continuously according to the target's changing position. Electronically, this meant feeding a signal from a sensor (something that monitors the environment) to an effector (something that makes a response, such as moving the gun barrel). As soon as the effector acts, the incoming information will also change (for example, the angle between the gun and plane will change). This is feedback.

Feedback can be either negative or positive. In negative feedback, the incoming information is used to correct the device's action continuously to minimize the difference between the incoming and outgoing information. If this works properly, the shells from the gun will converge on the position of the plane, destroying it. Positive feedback, on the other hand, responds to an input by increasing or diverging the output. An example is an amplifier that accentuates (and thus amplifies) an incoming wave signal. The "feedback" that sometimes makes an audio amplifier squeal when a musician gets too close is positive feedback.

## Computers and Controls

By the end of the war, the first electronic computers (such as ENIAC) were coming into use. While Wiener was involved only indirectly in computer development, he saw great potential for the computers as controllers for sophisticated machines such as communications signal processors. In a classified mathematical paper distributed widely to military researchers, Wiener pointed out that communications operations "carried out by electrical or mechanical or other such means, are in no way essentially different from the operations computationally carried out by . . . the computing machine."

Wiener also saw a broader application for the new computing technology. To encourage research, in December 1944, Wiener sent out a letter to mathematicians, experts in the emerging field of electronic computing, and neurophysiologists. The letter, calling for a two-day conference in Princeton, was signed by Wiener, pioneer computer designer Howard Aiken, and John von Neumann, a versatile mathematician who had helped design ENIAC. It explained that

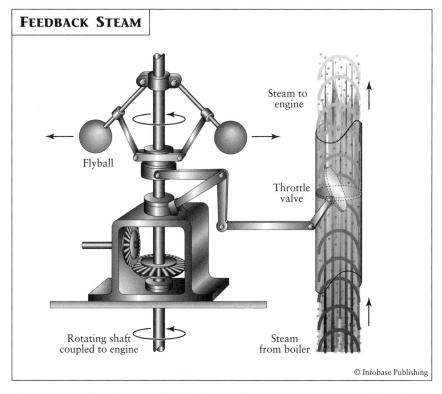

**FEEDBACK STEAM**

Steam to engine

Flyball

Throttle valve

Rotating shaft coupled to engine

Steam from boiler

© Infobase Publishing

*One of the earliest forms of feedback was the governor used to regulate the pressure in a steam engine. As the engine speed increased, the spinning balls drew farther apart. A linkage then squeezed the throttle valve, which reduced the amount of steam pressure, slowing the engine. If the engine was too slow, the process reversed and opened the throttle. The engine was thus kept near a constant speed.*

*A group of people interested in communication engineering, the engineering of computing machines, the engineering of control devices . . . and the communication and control aspects of the nervous system has come to a tentative conclusion that the relations between these fields of research have developed to a degree of intimacy that makes a get-together meeting between people interested in them highly desirable.*

## Neural Networks

While others worked on the organization of programs and data in computers, Wiener remained focused on communications and control. For him this meant how these processes were carried out by living things and the similarities between neurological and electronic structures.

Since the 1930s, Wiener had closely followed Arturo Rosenbleuth's work, particularly his study of nervous spasms involving a progressive loss of control. Rosenbleuth had found that in these conditions the nerve signals were not being accurately processed. Wiener realized that, similar to the antiaircraft gun that was slewing and unable to track the moving plane, these nerve circuits were suffering from feedback problems. The same principles that could be used to understand automatic control systems should also be applicable to neurology.

Rosenbleuth, together with Warren McCulloch (a leading neuropsychiatrist) and the logician Walter Pitts, had begun to develop a new mathematics to describe networks of nerve cells (neurons) that made up the brain's information processing systems. McCulloch and Pitts further demonstrated their theories by constructing the first "neural network," an electronic circuit whose components behave in ways similar to neurons.

Neural networks would help answer a difficult question: How does the brain make sense of the images created by the eyes' arrays of light-sensing cells? In other words, how does the brain recognize a pattern (such as the numeral "5") from the surrounding background? This research also helped validate Wiener's growing belief that a single framework could be applied to control and communication in living things, computers, and a coming generation of robots.

## Toward a New Science

As Wiener and his colleagues began to draw together their different strands of thought, they were aided greatly by a unique series

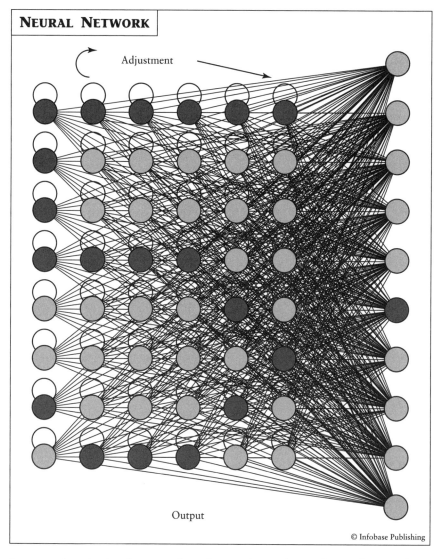

NEURAL NETWORK

Adjustment

Output

© Infobase Publishing

*In a neural network, a large number of processing nodes are "trained" to perform a task (such as recognizing a letter) by reinforcing correct responses.*

of conferences sponsored by the Josiah Macy Jr. Foundation, an organization devoted to improving medical education. The first meeting in 1942 cast the net wide, going beyond the physical sciences by bringing together psychologists, physiologists, and social scientists. Participants included Walter McCulloch, as well as the noted anthropologists Gregory Bateson and Margaret Mead. Arturo Rosenblueth brought Wiener's and his own ideas to the conference.

Rosenblueth suggested that a wide variety of biological and human communication processes needed to be understood not as simple cause-and-effect but rather as "circular causality"—feedback. This meant that action had an inherent purpose (such as maintaining an equilibrium or tracking sources of light or heat).

Meanwhile, Bateson sought to apply feedback theory to social interactions. Margaret Mead later observed in her 1968 paper "Cybernetics of Cybernetics" that she became so excited by this idea that "I did not notice that I had broken one of my teeth until the Conference was over."

Wiener proposed that a new group be formed to provide for the ongoing interdisciplinary study of communication, control, feedback, and other key concepts. He called the group the Teleological Society. Teleology is an approach to philosophy that focuses on the purpose or goal of a design or process. For example, instead of only studying how signals move between neurons in the visual cortex, a teleological approach looks at the organism's purposes or goals. What is the visual system (the eye and brain) "trying" to recognize? How does it go about adjusting or reinforcing the nerve signals in order to recognize, for example, a dangerous predator? (It should be noted that teleology as envisioned by Wiener does not mean conscious purpose; rather, it refers to the goals designed into the system, either by evolution or by human engineers.)

The Teleological Society had its first meeting at Princeton's Institute for Advanced Study on January 6 and 7, 1945. As he would report in his autobiography, Wiener was quite satisfied with these first proceedings:

> *Very shortly we found that people working in all these fields were beginning to talk the same language, with a vocabulary containing expressions from the communications engineer, the servomechanism man, the computing-machine man, and the neurophysiologist. . . . All*

*of them were interested in the storage of information. . . . All of them found that the term feedback . . . was an appropriate way of describing phenomena in the living organism as well as in the machine.*

## Cybernetics

By 1947, Wiener decided he was ready to bring his ideas to both the larger world of science and to the scientifically literate public. As he retired to Mexico City to write his book, Wiener was faced with a simple question: What should he call the new science he and his colleagues had been developing?

As he later wrote in his second autobiography:

*I first looked for a Greek word signifying "messenger," but the only one I knew was angelos (angel). . . . Then I looked for an appropriate word from the field of control. The only word I could think of was the Greek word for steersman, kubernetes.*

Weiner decided that the Greek steersman was a good analogy to the mechanisms about which he would be writing.

Published simultaneously in France and the United States in 1948, *Cybernetics* was not an easy book to understand. Nevertheless, the general public found intriguing ideas nestled among the math. The prestigious magazine *Scientific American* made the book its cover story, and *Newsweek* also featured it. Even at the end of the century, *Scientific American* would still consider *Cybernetics* to be one of the most "memorable and influential" works of 20th-century science. Wiener noted, though, in his second autobiography that "when [*Cybernetics*] became a scientific best-seller we were all astonished, not least myself."

Readers who persevered were rewarded with a comprehensive look at the ideas that would characterize the coming revolution in computers, communications, industrial technology, and robotics:

- The idea of information as a central and measurable quantity
- Information expressing the degree of organization of a system (making it the opposite of entropy, or disorder)

- "Control by informative feedback," where a machine is guided by the results of previous actions
- A balance between negative (self-correcting) and positive (amplifying) feedback
- The creation of communications networks and their analogy to nervous systems
- The broad applicability of cybernetics to fields ranging from computer science to sociology and psychology

In the 1950s and early 1960s, cybernetics became a sort of cultural phenomenon. It offered buzzwords for facile commentators but also potential areas of exploration for researchers in dozens of fields and applications.

## Cybernetics and Robotic Turtles

In the early 1950s, some practical applications of cybernetics aroused considerable interest. Grey Walter's "tortoise" robots, which were featured in *Scientific American,* demonstrated how a cybernetic system could be designed so that it interacted with its environment (through feedback) and exhibited lifelike behaviors. Primarily an analog rather than a digital device, the simple robot first checks for obstacles so it can change its direction of motion to avoid a collision. Just as humans do this automatically while walking, even while pursuing some higher goal (such as the refrigerator), Walter's tortoise had the "higher" goal of seeking and moving toward light sources. This movement was governed by several rules:

- If the area around the robot is dark, the robot searches for light and moves toward it if found.
- As long as the light level is moderate, the robot continues to move toward the light source.
- If the light becomes too bright, the robot reverses direction to avoid becoming "dazzled."

Depending on how the light sources in the room are arranged, the result is surprising, unpredictable behavior. Even with only a few

*Grey Walter's robotic tortoise used simple motors, relays, and a photocell to detect light. Nevertheless, its feedback circuits produced remarkably complex behavior, particularly when interacting with other tortoise robots.* (© Science and Society Picture Library)

sensors and switches, the tortoise robots seemed to behave in intricate ways. When lights were mounted on two robots, they began a sort of "mating dance." The cybernetic tortoise can be viewed as the first mobile robot to interact meaningfully with its environment.

## The Boston Arm

Another project had a more immediate practical use. For many years, Wiener had expressed an interest in designing mechanical aids or prostheses to help people who had lost a limb. In 1961, Wiener's interest was further piqued by comments made by his doctor while Wiener was hospitalized for a broken hip.

Early in the 20th century, leg prostheses were clumsy and uncomfortable, while artificial arms were barely useful for grasping. Wiener realized that since the human muscular system created electrical signals, there was no reason why signals from the stump could not be used to actuate a mechanical limb.

In the early 1960s, Wiener and MIT engineer Amar Bose designed a motorized arm that could be strapped to the wearer's remaining stump. Sensors placed above the point of amputation would pick up nerve signals and translate them to control signals to move the arm. By using what would later be called biofeedback training, the wearer could become increasingly dexterous in using the prostheses. The

---

**PARALLELS: APPLICATIONS OF CYBERNETICS**

In *Cybernetics*, Wiener had supplied what science historian Thomas Kuhn would later call a "paradigm"—a model that could provide a satisfying explanation for a group of phenomena. What was most unusual about cybernetics is that it was a sort of "super paradigm" that offered itself to many seemingly unrelated sciences and technologies. Some of the fields influenced by cybernetics include:

- Computer science—computer architecture, artificial intelligence, networking, and control applications
- Industrial automation—computer-controlled machines and, eventually, industrial robots
- Robotics—robots that can sense and interact with their environment
- Electronics—signal processing, amplification, and circuit design
- Information theory—the relationship between information and order
- Sociology—communication and information exchange within cultures
- Neurology and cognitive science—structure and function of the brain and nervous system
- Psychology—mental illness as a breakdown in information processing, communications, or feedback

Although the specific use of the word *cybernetics* has declined in recent decades, the underlying ideas remain important and have contributed to interdisciplinary advances such as the creation of new prosthetic devices.

project, which became known as the Boston Arm, was sponsored by MIT, Massachusetts General Hospital, the Harvard Medical School, and Liberty Mutual Insurance Company.

When the prototype arm was completed, it was attached to a volunteer amputee. As Bose recalled in Flo Conway and Jim Siegelman's biography of Norbert Wiener:

> We attached the arm—I can remember the reaction very clearly—the man was sitting down and the arm came up and he said, "My god, It's chasing me!" But in ten minutes time he was able to wear it beautifully.

## Facing the Social Consequences

Although the technological potential of cybernetics was exciting, during and after World War II, Wiener became increasingly concerned—even depressed—about what he saw as possible negative consequences of the new science.

Wiener's greatest concern about cybernetics was how a revolution in automation might affect society. In a 1946 conference at the New York Academy of Sciences, Wiener predicted that the computer will become the "central nervous system in future automatic-control machines." He also saw the eventual "coupling of human beings into a larger communication system."

But what would this mean for the world's economic or social life? Wiener noted that

> [Cybernetics] gives the human race a new and most effective collection of mechanical slaves to perform its labor. Such mechanical labor has most of the economic properties of slave labor, although unlike slave labor, it does not involve the direct demoralizing effects of human cruelty. However, any labor that accepts the conditions of competition with slave labor accepts the conditions of slave labor, and is essentially slave labor.

Wiener's remarks foresaw what would half a century later become a growing unease with the prospects of economic globalism—although the latter is focused more on the threat of cheap human labor.

Wiener did not see any way that the new technology could be undone or its development delayed significantly. As he warned in the introduction to *Cybernetics:*

*We can only hand [cybernetics] over into the world that exists about us, and this is the world of Belsen and Hiroshima. We do not even have the choice of suppressing these new technical developments. They belong to the age. . . . The best we can do is to see that a large public understands the trend and the bearing of the present work, and to confine our personal efforts to those fields . . . most remote from war and exploitation.*

Wiener retired from MIT in 1960. In 1964, he received the prestigious National Medal of Technology from President Lyndon Johnson. Wiener died on March 18, 1964, after collapsing suddenly while visiting Stockholm, Sweden.

By the time Wiener's productive career was ending, the first industrial robots were beginning to work on automobile assembly lines. Their more agile cousins would soon be scurrying along the corridors at MIT and other research institutions. Norbert Wiener had created a new conceptual framework for understanding such machines as well as the human brain and nervous system. He also left as a legacy a warning that the new machines would challenge people to treat each other as more, not less, human.

## Chronology

| | |
|---|---|
| **1894** | Norbert Wiener born November 26 in Columbia, Missouri |
| **1901** | Wiener enters elementary school and is placed with much older students. Dissatisfied, his father starts to educate him at home |
| **1905** | Wiener graduates from high school at the age of 11 |
| **1906** | Wiener is enrolled at Tufts College, where he is hailed as the youngest university student in the nation's history |

| | |
|---|---|
| **1909** | Wiener graduates from Tufts with a bachelor's degree in mathematics<br><br>Wiener enters Harvard to study zoology but does not do well |
| **1910** | Wiener switches to Cornell University and studies mathematics and philosophy; he soon returns to Harvard to pursue mathematics |
| **1912** | Wiener receives his master's degree in mathematics from Harvard and obtains his Ph.D. a year later |
| **1913** | Wiener begins to tour Europe, visiting prominent mathematicians |
| **1917** | As the United States enters World War I, Wiener does work in ballistics at the Aberdeen Proving Grounds |
| **1919** | Wiener accepts a faculty position at the Massachusetts Institute of Technology (MIT), where he will remain for the rest of his career |
| **1921** | Wiener publishes his first major mathematical paper, on Brownian motion |
| **1926** | Now an associate professor, Wiener marries Margaret Engemann, an assistant professor of modern languages |
| **1935** | Wiener lectures for two years at Tsing-Hua University in Beijing, China, forming an attachment to Chinese researchers |
| **1939** | World War II begins in Europe. Wiener helps with efforts to rescue Jewish scientists from the Nazis |
| **1945** | On January 6 and 7, Wiener's Teleological Society has its first meeting |
| **1948** | Wiener publishes *Cybernetics,* his most influential work |
| **1950** | Wiener increasingly turns his attention to the potential misuse of technology and automation. He publishes *The Human Use of Human Beings* |
| **1960** | Wiener retires from MIT and devotes his efforts to discussing the impact of technology on society |

| | |
|---|---|
| **1964** | MIT researchers develop an artificial arm based on Wiener's design |
| | Wiener receives the National Medal of Technology; he dies on March 18 in Stockholm, Sweden |

## Further Reading

### Books

Conway, Flo, and Jim Siegelman. *Dark Hero of the Information Age: In Search of Norbert Wiener, the Father of Cybernetics.* New York: Basic Books, 2005.
> A new and full biography that explores Wiener's tangled life and the significance of his work.

Wiener, Norbert. *Cybernetics: Or Control and Communication in the Animal and the Machine.* 2nd ed. Cambridge, Mass.: MIT Press, 1961.
> The book that defined and popularized cybernetics as a discipline.

———. *Ex-Prodigy: My Childhood and Youth.* Cambridge, Mass.: MIT Press, 1953.
> Wiener's account of his intellectual development and the emotional pressures of being raised as a "project" by his father.

———. *The Human Use of Human Beings.* 2nd ed. New York: Avon Books, 1970.
> Wiener's warnings about the economic and social consequences of automation.

———. *I Am a Mathematician: The Later Life of a Prodigy.* Garden City, N.Y.: Doubleday, 1956.
> Continues Wiener's autobiography and describes his career and the founding of the discipline of cybernetics.

### Article

Gasperi, Michael. "Grey Walter's Machina Speculatrix." Available online. URL: http://www.plazaearth.com/usr/gasperi/Walter.htm. Accessed on June 16, 2005.
> Describes Grey Walter's robot tortoises and their behavior. The site also includes some information about Lego Mindstorms robot kits and projects.

## Web Sites

**History of Cybernetics.** American Society for Cybernetics. URL: http://www.asc-cybernetics.org/foundations/historyrefs.htm. Accessed on September 20, 2005.
> Provides overview and resources for the history of cybernetics as a discipline.

**Principia Cybernetica Web.** URL: http://pespmc1.vub.ac.be. Accessed on September 25, 2005.
> Resource site from an international project devoted to developing a comprehensive philosophy of cybernetics.

# REVOLUTIONIZING INDUSTRY

## JOSEPH ENGELBERGER AND UNIMATE

In 1961, a new worker joined the General Motors assembly line in Turnstedt, New Jersey. The worker's job was to cast parts such as car doors from molten metal, give them a cooling dip in a vat of water, then handing them off to other workers who would trim and finish them. The worker belonged to no union, received no salary, and never needed a rest break. The worker was a robot called Unimate, and it revolutionized industry perhaps as much as powered machinery had done a century earlier. Unimate and later robots were largely the achievement of Joseph Engelberger, an engineer turned entrepreneur, and his partner, inventor George Devol.

## Hands-on Experience

Joseph Engelberger was born on July 26, 1925, in New York City. Engelberger recalled in a telephone interview with the author that his navy service in World War II was a career turning point. He became one of 14 candidates selected for the V12 program that paid for them to study physics (particularly nuclear physics) at Columbia University. Just after the war, Engelberger worked as an engineer on early nuclear tests such as at Bikini Atoll in the Pacific. He also worked on aerospace and nuclear power projects. After completing his military duties, Engelberger attended Columbia University's

School of Engineering and earned B.S. and M.S. degrees in physics and electrical engineering.

Engelberger said that he believes his grounding in physics served him well in his later work in developing robots that had to deal with the physical world. (Engelberger also expressed misgivings about modern researchers who think that "everything is software.")

## Developing Industrial Robots

During World War II, there had been tremendous progress in developing servomechanisms, or automatic controls, such as on the automatic gun turrets of the huge B-29 bomber. Servomechanisms allow for precise positioning and manipulation of parts of a machine. The rise of nuclear power and the need to handle radioactive materials safely also spurred the development of automatic controls. Engelberger's business ventures into this field included his starting a company called Consolidated Controls.

In the mid-1950s, Engelberger met George Devol, an inventor who had patented a programmable transfer machine. This was a device that could move components automatically from one specified position to another, such as in a die-casting machine that formed parts for automobiles.

Engelberger realized that Devol's machine could, with some additional

*Joseph Engelberger and inventor George Devol pioneered the development of industrial robotics, automating some of the most tedious and dangerous jobs on assembly lines. Here Engelberger is shown with Lab Mate, a robot used to prototype mobile helper robot applications.* (Photo courtesy of Joseph Engelberger)

extensions and capabilities, become a true robot. At Columbia, Engelberger had met Isaac Asimov, the science fiction writer whose robot stories have inspired several generations of robotics engineers. Starting in 1954, Devol concentrated on developing the new machine, called Unimate (for "Universal Automation"). Engelberger worked to raise business interest and obtain financing to manufacture the robots. In 1956, Engelberger and Devol founded Unimation, Inc.—the world's first industrial robot company.

Their robot, called Unimate, was—and is—essentially a large "shoulder" and arm. The shoulder can move along a track to position the arm near the materials to be manipulated. The arm can be equipped with a variety of specialized grasping "hands" to suit the task. The robot is programmed to perform a set of repetitive motions. It is also equipped with various devices for aligning the "work piece" (the object to be manipulated) and for making small adjustments in variations.

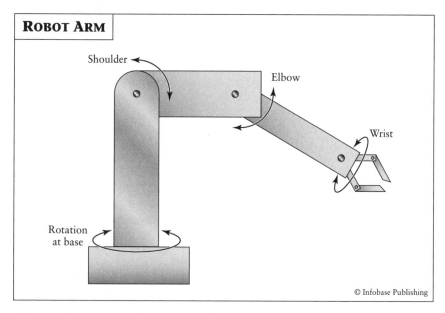

ROBOT ARM

Shoulder
Elbow
Wrist
Rotation at base

© Infobase Publishing

*A basic robotic manipulator arm, with joints equivalent to the base (torso), shoulder, elbow, and wrist of a person.*

**OTHER SCIENTISTS: GEORGE DEVOL (1920– )**

Much of the credit for the development of industrial robots goes to George Devol, a talented engineer and inventor. Born February 20, 1920, in Louisville, Kentucky, Devol was fascinated by mechanical and electronic engineering. Devol's first manufacturing efforts included phonograph arms, amplifiers, and an automatic "people counter" to tally attendance at the 1939 New York World's Fair.

In 1946, Devol patented a key device for industrial automation. It was a magnetic recorder that could store the details of mechanical motion. This meant that once a robot arm and gripper were "taught" how to perform a task by manually putting it through the motions, it could then "play back" the task over and over again, such as on an assembly line. As Devol noted in the patent application: "The present invention makes available for the first time a more or less general purpose machine that has universal application to a vast diversity of applications where cyclic control is desired."

In 1954, Devol built upon this principle to patent a robot called Unimate, short for "Universal Automation." In 1956, Devol got together with Joseph Engelberger to form Unimation, the first robot company. In later years, Devol also did important work in machine vision and bar-code processing.

## Robots on the Assembly Line

In the spring of 1961, the first Unimate robot began operations on the assembly line at the General Motors Plant in Turnstedt, a suburb of Trenton, New Jersey. Most of the factory's 3,000 human workers welcomed the newcomer. Unimate would be doing a job involving the casting of car doors and other parts from molten metal—hot, dangerous work. Steve Holland, chief scientist for manufacturing at General Motors, told *U.S. News & World Report* in 2003 that robots at first were mainly considered for "the three 'D' kinds of jobs. Jobs that are dirty, difficult, and dangerous." That first Unimate worked for nearly 10 years, keeping up tirelessly with three

*This Unimate robot is used for precision placement of fibers.* (Photo compliments of ADC Acquisition Co.)

shifts of human workers each day. This proven reliability would go a long way toward convincing industrialists about the value of robots on the assembly line.

The first industrial robots attracted modest public attention, but Engelberger found it hard at first to convince American investors and industrialists that robots were a good investment. By the mid-1960s, Unimation was demonstrating PUMA, a robot that had a more humanlike appearance than Unimate. The robot was shown to television viewers on *The Tonight Show* starring Johnny Carson. Engelberger recalled in an interview with the *Trentonian* that "The robot did a beer commercial and the people loved it. It took over the whole show. But after that, the only calls I got were from people who wanted my robot to be the entertainment at the county fair."

To this day, Engelberger is not impressed by toy robots that do cute tricks. As he told *Red Herring* magazine in 2000,

*The buyers of robotics wanted economic justification. So we studied 6 plants of Chrysler and 5 plants of Ford and 20 plants in Bridgeport, Connecticut. Out of that we built a spec. We said, "if we could build a device to meet this spec it would have broad utility in various jobs in industry." The hard fight was to convince someone to put the money up. We finally got financing, and finally got our first installation in 1961, which was a General Motors plant in Turnstedt, New Jersey. It served very well for many years and is now in the Smithsonian as the first industrial robot. From there it's been a long fight to convince people.*

## Industrial Robots Today

Today's industrial robots undertake a wider variety of jobs for which they are more efficient and less costly than human workers. Common applications include materials handling (moving parts from one assembly station to another), spot welding, and painting. In 2003 alone, manufacturing companies in the United States bought about $877 million worth of industrial robots—a 19 percent increase over the previous year's total. The automobile industry is still the leading user of robots, purchasing about two-thirds of the units sold in 2003.

While even Unimate's successors have little in the way of true artificial intelligence, they are more flexible and versatile than their predecessors. For example, a robot called C-Flex can identify different models of cars and perform different types of welding operations depending on which vehicle is passing on the assembly line.

Robots working in lighter industrial settings include machines that use their vision system to identify the tops and bottoms of Oreo cookies on the assembly line and then match them together at rates of up to 2,000 cookies per minute. (No human could do this job so quickly, and probably no human would *want* such a job.)

As the costs of human labor (including such expenses as health insurance) continue to rise, it seems likely that industrial robots will find their way into many more applications in coming decades. McDonald's has already tested a robotic burger-flipping machine. Some libraries have reconfigured their shelving so robot pages can fetch books on demand.

## SOCIAL IMPACT: ROBOTS AND HUMAN LABOR

The growing use of industrial robots in the United States has inevitably raised the question of what their impact will be on the jobs and pay of human workers. Joseph Engelberger has always claimed that robots have improved conditions for labor. In an interview with the *Trentonian*, Engelberger recalled that "There was very little opposition to robotics from American labor. It helped with working people that the first robots were put to work doing hot, hazardous and dull labor." Engelberger has suggested that the appropriate response to people losing their jobs to robots is retraining.

Workers have feared automation since the beginning of the industrial age. (In the late 18th century, the British followers of Ned Lud—the "Luddites"—broke into factories and destroyed machines.) This fear is not unreasonable: If a person has limited skills and performs repetitive work, his or her job description matches the strengths of robots. Robots can perform this kind of work to a high degree of consistency and, if necessary, can work three shifts a day. And while robots do require maintenance, they do not get sick nor do they require expensive health care. In some cases, robots may displace human workers entirely, while in others the availability of robots might depress the wages of human workers who have to compete with them.

In a way, robotlike devices have already displaced many service workers. Many people can fulfill their banking needs at an ATM and

# Robots in Service

In 1980, Engelberger published *Robotics in Practice*. This book and *Robotics in Service* (1989) became standard textbooks that defined the growing robotics industry by translating Engelberger's practical experience into workable approaches. The two titles also marked a shifting of Engelberger's focus from industrial robots to service robots—robots that function in workplaces such as warehouses or hospitals.

In 1982, Unimation was acquired by Westinghouse. By then Engelberger had founded Transitions Research Corporation, which

have not seen a human teller for years. Many supermarkets and libraries are installing self-checkout machines. According to Marshall Brain, author of "Robotic Nation," it is these specialized robotic machines that will have the real impact on workers. They will be followed by more sophisticated walking humanoid robots that might take over such jobs as receptionist, museum guide, store greeter, or even security guard. Brain predicts that by 2055 robots will have practically taken over the workplace. Their development will be driven by Moore's Law—the observation that computer power roughly doubles every two years.

Whether the threat is robots or cheaper foreign labor, there would seem to be three possible responses on the part of society. The first is to somehow stop the influx of the cheaper labor into the workplace. This seems unlikely to happen, in particular because the interests that most benefit from cheaper labor are politically influential. The second possibility is that enough new jobs will arise that require skills that are beyond the capability of robots. New technologies do bring new opportunities—look at all the jobs created in Internet and Web development and in venues such as eBay, despite the "dot-bust" early in the new century. But it is far from clear that enough such jobs can be created and that people can be retrained to do them. (People who work in the kinds of jobs that are likely to be automated are also more likely to lack sufficient educational background for more sophisticated jobs.) The last possibility is that our society and economy might be fundamentally restructured so that most people no longer need to work in order to live.

in 1984 became HelpMate Robotics, Inc. The company's most successful product has been the HelpMate hospital robot. The robot is designed to dispatch records, specimens, and supplies throughout a busy hospital. The robot received extensive field testing thanks to an arrangement with Danbury Hospital in Connecticut.

Automatic delivery vehicles are nothing new, but the HelpMate robot and its successors are much more flexible and capable. HelpMate does not follow a fixed track. Rather, it is programmed to visit a succession of areas or stations and to make its own way, using cameras to detect and go around obstacles. HelpMate can even summon an elevator to go to a different floor!

Along with other robotics entrepreneurs, Engelberger has pointed out in interviews with the author and others that he is also looking toward a time when robots will be able to perform a number of useful tasks in the home. In particular, Engelberger sees great potential

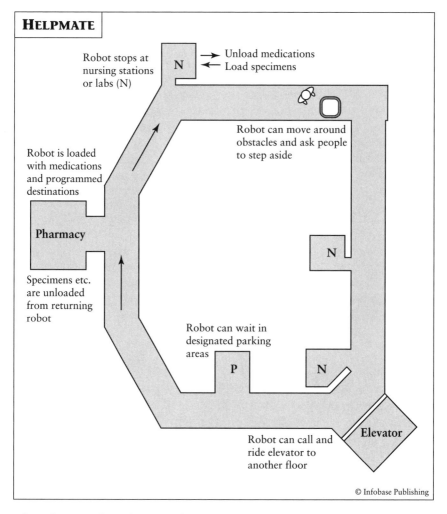

*This schematic shows how a HelpMate robot can deliver and pick up materials in a hospital. If necessary, the robot will even politely ask persons to step aside so it can move.*

for robots in helping to care for the growing population of elderly people who need assistance in the tasks of daily life. He points out that no government or insurance company can afford to hire a full-time human assistant to enable older people to continue living at home. A suitable robot could fetch things, remind a person when it is time to take medication, and even perform medical monitoring and summon help if necessary.

## Elder Statesperson of Robotics

Joseph Engelberger's achievements in industrial and service robotics have won him numerous plaudits and awards, including the Leonardo da Vinci Award of the American Society of Mechanical Engineers, the Progress Award of the Society of Manufacturing Engineers, the Japan Prize, and Columbia University's Egleston Medal. Engelberger was elected to the National Academy of Engineering in 1984. He has also received honorary doctorates from five institutions, including Carnegie Mellon University in Pittsburgh—one of the great centers of robotics research in the United States.

In 1992, Engelberger was included in the London *Sunday Times* series on "The 1000 Makers of the 20th Century." In 2000, Engelberger delivered the keynote address to the World Automation Congress, which was also dedicated to him. In 2004, he received the IEEE Robotics and Automation Award.

Since 1977, the Robotics Industries Association has presented the prestigious annual Joseph F. Engelberger Awards to honor the most significant innovators in the science and technology of robotics.

## A Wrong Direction?

Engelberger continues to have strong opinions about the future of the robotics industry and robotics research. At a time when many researchers are making robots that look increasingly like human beings, Engelberger focuses on functionality rather than appearance. As he told *Red Herring* magazine in 2000,

*I want to make a robot that is in the image of the principles set out by my mentor, Isaac Asimov. The model is the human being. It doesn't have to look like a human being. It doesn't have to be physically the same, but it has to operate in our environment and use our data and our tools. And that is the challenge. That is where the robot will break out.*

Engelberger went on to tell *Red Herring* that he thinks much of the work of academic robotics researchers in trying to give robots humanlike qualities is on the wrong track:

*It sounds nice to have a robot that can recognize gestures. But language is so powerful. Tell the robot what you want. If a robot can read sign language, then it can cope with input from a deaf person. The research community has been very sad in its ability to do things. When I see MIT working on giving a robot face emotion, I say, "What the hell is going on? Who cares about the robot's emotion? I want to know what it's doing." Why is that? Because maybe someone got a Ph.D. for making the robot smile and frown. But really what they should have made it do is cook and clean.*

---

### TRENDS: THE ROBOTICS INDUSTRY TODAY

According to the 2004 World Robotics Survey by the United Nations Economic Commission for Europe, the robotics industry is booming. In 2004, orders for industrial robots increased 18 percent, reaching the highest level ever recorded. There are now at least 800,000 industrial robots in use (see pie chart). Japan became the world leader in robotics in the 1980s, but the rest of the industrialized world has been rapidly catching up.

Meanwhile, robots are also entering the home, with 600,000 in use by 2004 and several million more likely to be purchased in the next few years.

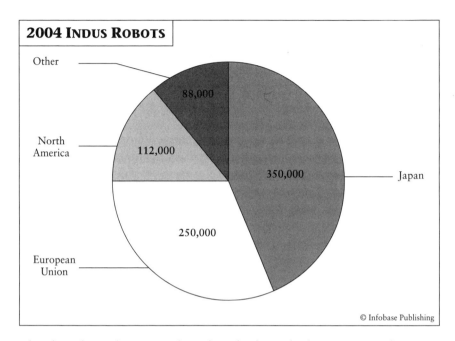

**2004 INDUS ROBOTS**

Other — 88,000

North America — 112,000

Japan — 350,000

European Union — 250,000

© Infobase Publishing

*This chart shows the estimated number of industrial robots in use as of 2004.*
(Source: United Nations Economic Commission for Europe.)

Similarly, according to an article in Robotics Online, Engelberger is not impressed by walking robots, let alone hopping or running ones. He believes wheels are quite adequate for most of the applications where robots are actually economically justified. Engelberger argues that industry experts should formulate realistic, real-world goals for robotics research, focusing on practical service applications and the creation of "personal robots."

# Chronology

| | |
|---|---|
| **1925** | Joseph Engelberger born July 26 in New York City |
| **1946** | Engelberger graduates from Columbia University School of Engineering |
| **1954** | George Devol invents a programmable industrial robot |

| 1956 | Devol and Engelberger found Unimation, Inc. |
|------|---------------------------------------------|
| 1957 | Engelberger founds Consolidated Controls Corporation in Danbury, Connecticut |
| 1961 | An industrial robot (Unimate) is installed for the first time on a production line, at General Motors |
| 1966 | A robot appears on *The Tonight Show* starring Johnny Carson, demonstrating bartending, golfing, and music skills |
| 1977 | The Robotics Industry Association establishes the Joseph Engelberger Award for outstanding achievement in robotics |
| 1980 | Engelberger publishes *Robotics in Practice* |
| 1982 | Unimation is acquired by Westinghouse. Engelberger soon leaves the firm and founds Transition Research Corporation |
| 1984 | Engelberger founds HelpMate Robotics, Inc. |
| 1989 | Engelberger publishes *Robotics in Service* |
| 1999 | HelpMate Robotics is acquired by Cardinal Health |
| 2000 | Engelberger gives the keynote speech at the World Automation Congress |
| 2003 | About $877 million worth of industrial robots are purchased in the United States alone |

# Further Reading

## Books

Engelberger, Joseph F. *Robotics in Practice: Management and Applications of Industrial Robots.* New York: AMACOM, 1980.
In this textbook of industrial robotics, Engelberger gives a nod to his mentor by including a foreword by Isaac Asimov.
———. *Robotics in Service.* Cambridge, Mass.: MIT Press, 1989.
Reflects Engelberger's later focus on service robots in nonindustrial workplaces, including technology for obstacle sensing and navigation and a survey of 15 possible application areas.

Nof, Shimon Y. *Handbook of Industrial Robotics*. 2nd ed. New York: Wiley, 1999.

> Both a handbook and an extensive resource guide to the state of the art in industrial robotics, with contributions from 120 leading experts from 12 countries.

## Articles

Brain, Marshall. "Robotic Nation." Available online. URL: http://marshallbrain.com/robotic-nation.htm. Accessed on September 26, 2005.

> Describes how robots and other automatic systems are rapidly displacing human workers in service jobs.

Engelberger, Joseph. "Whatever Became of Robotics Research." Robotics Online. Available online. URL: http://www.roboticsonline.com/public/articles/articlesdetails.cfm?id=769. Accessed on July 28, 2005.

> Engelberger argues for a more practical focus for robotics research.

Mickle, Paul. "1961: A Peep into the Automated Future." *Trentonian*. The Capital Century, 1900–99. Available online. URL: http://www.capitalcentury.com/1961.html. Accessed on August 30, 2005.

> Describes the first Unimate robot and how people in Trenton, New Jersey, reacted to it in 1961, as well as later developments.

Pethokoukis, James M., Margaret Mannix, and Tim Smart. "Meet Your New Co-Worker." *U.S. News & World Report* 136 (March 15, 2004): EE2 ff.

> Describes how robots are used today, using as an example a manufacturing plant in Illinois. Also discusses the economics of industrial automation.

"Mr. Roboto." *Red Herring,* August 1, 2000. Available online. URL: http://www.redherring.com/Article.aspx?a=7597&hed=Mister+Roboto#. Accessed on August 15, 2005.

> Engelberger assesses the achievements and shortcomings of current robotics research.

## Web Site

**Robotics Online.** http://www.roboticsonline.com. Accessed on October 18, 2005.

> Site sponsored by the Robotics Industry Association; provides news and background information on the robotics industry and gives the annual Joseph F. Engelberger Awards for excellence in robotics.

# 3

# LEARNING TO WALK

## MARC RAIBERT AND ROBOTS WITH LEGS

---

Many robots in science fiction movies walk like people, striding along confidently. But most real-world mobile robots (such as those that deliver prescriptions in hospitals) roll along on wheels. It is not easy to get a robot to master walking, a skill that humans learn as toddlers. But there are some very good reasons to make robots that can walk or run.

In a 1986 article for *Communications of the ACM*, the journal of the Association for Computing Machinery, robotics engineer Marc Raibert pointed out:

*There is a need for vehicles that can travel in difficult terrain, where existing vehicles cannot go. Wheels excel on prepared surfaces such as rails and roads, but perform poorly where the terrain is soft or uneven. Because of these limitations, only about half the earth's landmass is accessible to existing wheeled and tracked vehicles, whereas a much greater area can be reached by animals on foot. It should be possible to build legged vehicles that can go to the places that animals can now reach.*

Raibert went to explain a key reason why legs can be better than wheels:

*One reason legs provide better mobility in rough terrain is that they can use isolated footholds that optimize support and traction, whereas a wheel requires a continuous path of support. As a consequence, a legged system can choose among the footholds in the reachable terrain; a wheel must negotiate the worst terrain. A ladder illustrates this point: Rungs provide footholds that enable the ascent of legged systems, but the spaces between rungs prohibit the ascent of wheeled systems.*

Additionally, Raibert pointed out that with legs, the main body (and whatever it is carrying) can move independently of the propulsion system—thus a pizza delivery person can walk up stairs while keeping the pie level. Finally, of course, with legs, one can step over obstacles that would stop a wheeled cart in its tracks.

## Making of an Engineer

Marc Raibert was born in New York City in 1949. He graduated from Northeastern University with a bachelor's degree in electrical engineering in 1973, receiving a doctorate from the Massachusetts Institute of Technology (MIT) in 1977. Raibert then worked at the Jet Propulsion Laboratory (JPL) in Pasadena, California, as a staff engineer from 1977 to 1980. JPL was (and is) the nation's foremost center of research and development in space robotics, including planetary probes and rovers. Working there spurred Raibert's interest in finding better ways for robots to move across terrain.

In 1981, Raibert went to Carnegie Mellon University, where he was an associate professor of computer science and robotics until 1986. Raibert established the Leg Laboratory for the study of legged robot locomotion. He then went to MIT, taking

*Marc Raibert's research has drawn on animal locomotion to develop legged robots that can walk, hop, and even run dynamically.* (Photo courtesy of Marc Raibert)

the Leg Laboratory with him. Raibert served as a professor of electrical engineering and computer science at MIT until 1995.

## Dynamic Walkers

In the 1980s, legged locomotion was one of the largest undeveloped frontiers in robotics. Progress had been slow. Inventors had experimented with walking machines as early as the 19th century. These machines could only place legs in sequence stiffly and mechanically, without regard to obstacles or uneven terrain.

In the 1970s, computer control began to be applied to creating more sophisticated walking machines. For example, in 1977, Robert McGhee at Ohio University led the successful development of an insect-like hexapod (six-legged) walker that could climb stairs. In 1980, Japanese researchers built a four-legged machine that used more sophisticated computer algorithms to enable it to negotiate obstacles.

This first generation of computerized walkers had a fundamental characteristic in common. They were "static crawlers." Such machines balanced by keeping most of their feet on the ground. As a leg moved forward, the center of mass remained balanced over the stationary legs. While this kept the robot stable at all times, it also meant that the robot lacked the agility of a walking human. In an article published in 2001 in *Science News,* Raibert recalled that early walking robots were "like tables with moving legs."

As Raibert had noted earlier in a 1990 article in *U.S. News & World Report,* "Biology already has the solutions—if we can tease them out." Consider how people walk. People have only two legs, so they cannot remain balanced in a static way while moving forward. Indeed, people sort of fall forward with each step, accelerating. We do not fall over because part of us tips backward at the same time, compensating and keeping an overall balance.

Raibert pointed out that there are important advantages to this dynamic form of locomotion. For one thing, with no need to keep rigidly over our center of mass, we can vary how far apart our feet are placed—for example, to avoid rocks while hiking along a path.

Walking is a pendulum-like motion, and back in the 1950s, famed computer scientist Claude Shannon, Robert Cannon, and the latter's graduate students at Stanford University experimented with

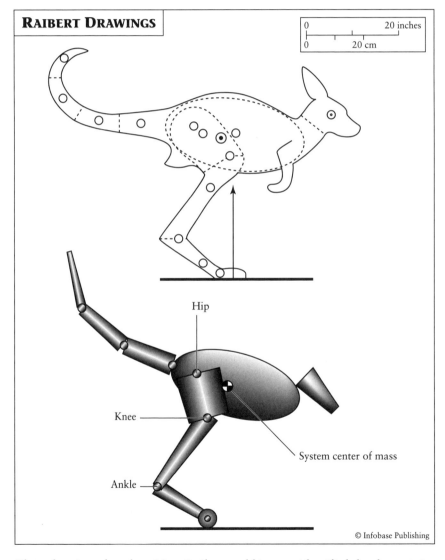

*These drawings show how Marc Raibert and his team identified the elements in a kangaroo's hopping gait and determined the location of the center of mass.*

upside-down pendulums mounted on moving carts. They developed mathematical equations that specified the ranges of motion in which balance could be maintained.

Using related ideas, Ralph Mosher at General Electric developed walking devices that would be controlled by a human operator. The operator would be placed in a harness such that his or her walking motions would be translated into powered walking movement by the machine. In 1968, Mosher demonstrated his "walking truck" for the military.

## Robot Kangaroos

Building a dynamic walking robot involves several different systems. Besides controlling the specific motion of each leg joint, some sort of master controller must determine the sequence in which the legs move. In turn, these instructions must take account of feedback that informs the robot when it is getting out of balance (and in what direction). Finally, there has to be a sort of "strategic planner" that determines the robot's desired destination, examines possible footholds (places to step down), and picks the best route.

Raibert and his team at the Leg Laboratory began with a very simple proof-of-concept: a robot "pogo stick." It consisted of a computer-controlled piston that determined how far the robot could stride forward without losing its balance and another control that determined how much "spring" or "bounce" could propel the leg from one stride to the next. By combining legs, Raibert and his team later built two-legged (bipedal) and four-legged (quardapedal) robots.

They got their idea for the robot from one of nature's most accomplished hoppers: the kangaroo! They studied the structure of the animal's bones and muscles and analyzed its hopping gait.

One special thing about Raibert's approach is that it did not require exhaustive calculations or some sort of central control system. As long as each leg (or coordinated leg pair) was kept in balance, the robot as a whole remained in balance. Nevertheless, the filmed trials of the robots include blooper reels featuring the worst stumbles and crashes of the early prototypes. But progress continued. By 1984, a quadrupedal robot could trot across the laboratory floor. A year later, a more humanlike bipedal machine could run while changing gaits. This improvement reflected a growing understanding of the fundamental elements involved in legged locomotion.

Raibert's approach breaks the process into three forms of control. Consider again how people run. Part of the energy is expended for a sort of hopping motion, pushing the leg like a spring to overcome the force of gravity. Meanwhile, legs are alternately moved forward. While this is going on, the body also has to maintain an appropriate posture, controlling the angle between the trunk and legs and remaining upright.

The design of the running robot involved creating a computer algorithm for each of the three kinds of motion—upward, forward, and postural. This is a simpler task than trying to control everything

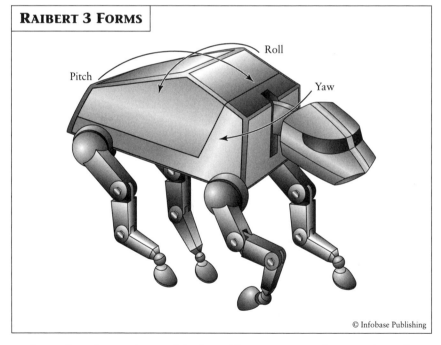

**RAIBERT 3 FORMS**

Roll

Pitch

Yaw

© Infobase Publishing

*Raibert's three forms of control for legged locomotion are shown with a robot quadraped. The three motions to be adjusted are forward (roll), up and down (pitch), and tilting (yaw).*

at once. The algorithms could then be fine-tuned to synchronize the three aspects of motion under a wide range of conditions.

The simplest form of locomotion is where only one leg moves at a time. To walk like a human or a cat, however, it is necessary to have more than one leg moving simultaneously. Raibert solved this problem by combining two or even four legs into a single "virtual leg," where the individual legs are coordinated so they act like the simpler single leg model.

## Boston Dynamics

Practical walking robots would have to have far more extensive capabilities than those in the Leg Lab's simple walking demonstrations. In the real world, robots would have to navigate around furniture and people . . . or clamber over rock-strewn terrain. Vision systems and artificial intelligence would be needed for the robot to "know" how to adjust its stride to fit the kind of surface it was traveling over.

In 1992, Raibert began to move from the academic world to the realm of industry. He became president of an innovative software company called Boston Dynamics. The company specialized in simulations of human movement for the government and military.

In particular, Raibert applied his concepts of robot motion to the problem of generating realistic animated simulations of motion for simulations, games, and even movies. Using his software, a special-effects designer would not have to animate each tiny stage painstakingly in the motion of, for example, a dinosaur. He or she could simply set the necessary parameters, tell the software where the dinosaur should move on the screen, and have the animation sequence generated automatically.

Using a product called Di-Guy, makers of games and simulations can easily add lifelike human characters. The product has become quite popular with the military, which can use pre-built characters, including various types of soldiers and specialists such as landing signal officers and "first responders," complete with protective masks and other gear.

## CONNECTIONS: BEASTS AND BOTS

Scientists and engineers since the time of Leonardo da Vinci (1452–1519) have studied biological anatomy and often tried to incorporate its principles in building such things as flying machines. Generally, it has turned out that direct imitation of nature's mechanisms has not worked well with machines—thus airplanes do not fly the way birds do, although aspects of their wing structure are similar.

In building robots (sometimes colloquially called "bots") that have more of the capabilities of animals and people, today's researchers have studied creatures ranging from the cockroach to dogs and even kangaroos. But at the same time that nature may be teaching the engineer, the engineer may also be helping to unlock the secrets of nature. As Raibert pointed out in his 1986 article, "Legged Robots," in *Communications of the ACM:*

> One way to learn more about plausible mechanisms for animal loco-motion is to build legged machines. To the extent that an animal and a machine perform similar locomotion tasks, their control systems and mechanical structures must solve similar problems. By building machines, we can gain new insights into these problems and learn about possible solutions.

Another way to look at the possible convergence of biological and mechanical systems of control and locomotion is to consider how evolution has often guided different types of creatures to develop similar structures for similar tasks. (For example, insects, birds, and even mammals [bats] all developed wings for flight). In a way, robots, too, may be "evolving" similar structures to fit the niches or applications in which they will increasingly be found in the future.

Just as Raibert found that relatively simple overall adjustments (such as changing stride length and posture) were enough to maintain balance while running, animal research is now suggesting that the nervous system does not "micromanage" locomotion but instead uses relatively simple overall controls. As Raibert told Stephen Budiansky, "the mechanical system has a mind of its own."

## Robot Mules

An important early advance in many civilizations was the use of beasts of burden such as horses, mules, oxen, and camels to carry goods. In the past few years, Raibert has been a key researcher in a project to create the mechanical equivalent of the mule. Called "BigDog," a prototype walking robot offers the military the ability to increase the carrying capacity of infantry. The robot

---

### SOLVING PROBLEMS: ROBOTS AND ANIMATION

In 1872, photographer Eadweard Muybridge (1830–1904) set up a series of cameras at a racetrack. Each camera was set up so that as a galloping horse passed, a cord would break and a picture would be taken. The result was the first photographic study that revealed the exact sequence in which the legs of the horse moved. If one takes enough such pictures in rapid succession the result is a "moving picture"—a movie.

While film can be used to "decompose" walking or running into discrete movements, traditional animation is the reverse process. It attempts to create smooth action from a series of discrete images. There have been many approaches to animation, ranging from cartoons with hand-painted frames (cels) to computer animation that uses algorithms to create smooth transitions from one defined "key frame" to the next.

The ultimate problem for animators is how to turn discrete images into smooth, realistic motion. One approach commonly used is to capture the motions of live human actors and incorporate them into the animation model. Unfortunately, the ability to integrate such captured motion smoothly is limited—fundamentally, because the modeler lacks real understanding of the mechanics and dynamics. Without knowing why things move the way they do, the ability to determine where they should move next is limited.

One of Raibert's key insights is that the same algorithms that enabled his robots to walk or run smoothly and realistically could also

dog—or perhaps better, "mule"—will be capable of intelligently finding its way around the terrain as it follows troops in combat. Able to carry supplies and ammunition, such robots could extend the range and duration of combat patrols in areas where vehicles are either not available or unable to clamber over terrain, such as the mountains of Afghanistan. (In addition to Boston Dynamics, the BigDog development team includes MIT, Harvard, and Stanford.)

be used to generate animation sequences. This worked by creating a "virtual robot" and subjecting it to real-world physics while simulating real-world mechanics. In a 1991 paper for the ACM *Computer Graphics* journal, Raibert and IBM researcher Jessica Hodgins explained how they constructed animation models for bipeds (running and hopping), quadrupeds (trotting, bounding, and galloping), and even kangaroo-style hopping. As with the original robot models, the general approach was to simplify the system by focusing on a single moving leg or coupled pair of legs. A leg is modeled as rigid segments connected by joints. Much of the complexity arises from dealing with the way energy is stored and released by muscles (actuators) and transformed via the joints, as well as accounting for the "springlike" characteristics of the feet as they contact and release from the ground.

Since that original work, great advances in computer power and the availability of many other sophisticated animation models (such as for human facial expressions) have combined to enable products from Boston Dynamics and other companies to include highly realistic portrayals of the human body under many different types of conditions.

The connections between legged robot locomotion, motion simulation, and animation are a striking illustration of how traditionally distinct fields such as biology, mechanical engineering, and computer graphics can develop together by tapping into a growing body of physical understanding. The results are likely to include more useful and versatile robots as well as educational simulations and games with greater accuracy and realism.

In designing the robot, Raibert noted to David Hambling of the British newspaper the *Guardian* that "There are tradeoffs with speed, the roughness of the terrain, and the payload." To be useful for its military application, the robot must be able to travel fast enough to keep up with the pace of marching soldiers. At the same time, it must be able to carry enough supplies to be worthwhile. So far the prototype BigDog has been able to climb a steep 30-degree slope while carrying a load of more than 110 pounds (50 kg.) As development continues, there are likely to be faster robots as well as specialized versions for scouting and rescue work.

An alternative way to help people carry big loads is to build robotic extensions to their own legs. In Robert Heinlein's novel *Starship Troopers,* soldiers of the future have powered suits that let them leap hundreds of yards and carry wounded comrades easily to safety. The Defense Advanced Research Projects Agency has announced a project for developing powered "exoskeletons" that would enable soldiers to carry hundreds of pounds.

Finally, Boston Dynamics' growing robot menagerie now includes RHex, a remote-controlled robot that can climb or clamber over any terrain and even swim and dive in swampy environments. The company has an even more remarkable climbing robot, the six-legged RiSE, which can climb straight up a wall, fence, or tree. These robots feature a variety of adaptations for dealing with different types of surfaces.

# A Dynamic Future

The best testament to Marc Raibert's more than 25 years of research into legged and other mobile robots is seen in the robots and animation products from Boston Dynamics, as well as in the industry as a whole. Thanks to Raibert and other researchers (such as the developers of Honda's Asimo robot), walking robots are making their sure-footed way into applications ranging from planetary exploration to entertainment.

Raibert has been a featured speaker at many robotics conferences, including the 25th anniversary conference on "Robots and Thought" sponsored by Carnegie Mellon University in 2004.

Raibert's main focus these days is in the business world, where he is devoted to the further development of a variety of mobile robot designs and applications, as well as innovative animation and simulation software.

## Chronology

| | |
|---|---|
| **1870** | Early walking machines are developed, but they can only walk stiffly and in a straight line |
| **1872** | Eadweard Muybridge begins photographic studies of locomotion in 40 different animals |
| **1949** | Marc Raibert born in New York City |
| **1968** | Ralph Mosher's prototype "walking truck" is tested by the U.S. Army |
| **1973** | Raibert graduates from Northeastern University with a degree in electrical engineering |
| **1977** | Raibert earns his doctorate at MIT<br><br>A computer-controlled six-legged (hexapod) robot is developed by Robert McGhee's group at Ohio State University |
| **1977–80** | Raibert works for three years as an engineer at the Jet Propulsion Laboratory in Pasadena, California |
| **1980** | Japanese researchers build a four-legged (quadrapedal) machine that can climb stairs |
| **1981** | Raibert becomes an associate professor of computer science and robotics at Carnegie Mellon University; he establishes the "Leg Laboratory" for research on walking robots |
| **1982** | Raibert's first hopping robot moves in place and can keep its balance |
| **1983** | A one-legged hopping robot runs and balances on an open floor |
| **1984** | Balancing techniques are successfully applied to a quadrupedal robot, which can then trot |

| | |
|---|---|
| **1986** | Raibert moves to MIT, along with the Leg Laboratory |
| | A two-legged (bipedal) robot can do flips and other acrobatics |
| **1989** | A bipedal robot jumps through a hoop |
| **1991** | A kangaroo-like robot hops, using an articulated leg and tail |
| | Raibert coauthors a paper that applies robot models to animation |
| **1992** | Raibert becomes president of Boston Dynamics, seeking to apply his robotics studies to animation |
| **1995** | Raibert leaves MIT and becomes president of Boston Dynamics |
| **2005** | Boston Dynamics offers "Di-Guy" software providing realistic human modeling for simulations |
| | The Defense Department funds ongoing research in walking "mule" robots to carry supplies for soldiers |

# Further Reading

## Books

Raibert, Marc. *Legged Robots That Balance*. Reprint. Boston: MIT Press, 2000.
> Describes the principles, implementation, and simulation of dynamic legged locomotion, including single-legged, bipedal, and quadrupedal machines.

## Articles

Budiansky, Stephen. "The Scientist Who Dances with Robots." *U.S. News & World Report* 117, 14 November 1990, n.p.
> Popular introduction to Marc Raibert's work with robots at the MIT Leg Laboratory.

Hambling, David. "A Breed Apart: Robots Could Yet Hit the Big Time, Now That the Pentagon Has Set Its Sights on the Four-Legged Variety." *Guardian,* February 24, 2005, n.p. Available online. URL: http://

technology.guardian.co.uk/online/insideit/story/0,13270,1423657, 00.html. Accessed September 4, 2005.
> Describes BigDog, LittleDog, and other robots being developed for military applications.

Pratt, Gill A. "Legged Robots at MIT—What's New Since Raibert." Reproduced from *Proceedings of the 1999 International Conference of Climbing and Walking Robots* 199. Available online. URL: http://www.uwe.ac.uk/clawar/newsletters/issue4/mit. html. Accessed on September 1, 2005.
> Describes further development of walking robots at MIT after Raibert's departure, including use of new forms of actuators and control mechanisms.

Raibert, Marc. "Legged Robots." *Communications of the ACM* 29 (June 1986): 499–514.
> Describes the utility of walking robots and the principles behind their operation.

———, and Jessica K. Hodgins. "Animation of Dynamic Legged Locomotion." *ACM Computer Graphics* 25 (July 1991): 349–358.
> Describes the innovative application of research into animal and robot locomotion to the creation of animations.

Weiss, Peter. "Hop . . . Hop . . . Hopbots!: Designers of Small, Mobile Robots Take Cues from Grasshoppers and Frogs." *Science News,* February 10, 2001, n.p. Available online. URL: http://www.find articles.com/p/articles/mi_m1200/is_6_159/ai_72058401. Accessed on September 3, 2005.
> Describes highly mobile robots inspired by watching grasshoppers' agile evasion tactics. NASA is adapting the technology to designing new Mars rovers.

## Web Sites

**Boston Dynamics.** URL: http://www.bostondynamics.com. Accessed on September 6, 2005.
> Presents digital motion simulation and modeling products, including "Di-Guy" package.

**MIT Leg Laboratory.** URL: http://www.ai.mit.edu/projects/leglab. Accessed on September 1, 2005.
> Describes the people and projects underway at the Massachusetts Institute of Technology's "Leg Laboratory."

# 4

# REAL-WORLD ROBOTS

## COLIN ANGLE, HELEN GREINER, AND iROBOT

Although the first electronic digital computers appeared in the mid-1940s, they would be confined for the next 30 years to big corporations, government agencies, and universities. Even when desktop personal computers first arrived in the 1970s, most people considered them to be novelties or toys for adventurous electronics hobbyists. Today, though, the personal computer in all its forms is nearly as commonplace as the television and telephone. The explosion in personal computing happened not only because the machines became increasingly powerful, inexpensive, compact and versatile but also because of compelling applications such as word processing, e-mail, and the World Wide Web.

Household robots are at a stage of development similar to that of the early days of the PC. Industrial robots have worked in factories since the 1970s, and experimental robots have rolled and walked through research labs, testing theories of artificial intelligence and interacting with people in increasingly sophisticated ways. But where is "Rosie," the housekeeping robot from the old *Jetsons* television show? The robot that can clean the house, do the dishes, take out the trash, and even babysit while the parents have a night out?

Such robots remain far in the future. But thanks to pioneer inventor-entrepreneurs Colin Angle and Helen Greiner of iRobot Corporation (and their colleague and mentor Rodney Brooks) more than a million robots were at work in American households by 2005, with growing numbers appearing in other countries as well. Right now, they are only cleaning the floor. But tomorrow a robot menagerie may take over many of the time-consuming tasks of daily life, while making homes safer and more responsive to peoples' needs.

## Hands-on Builder

Colin Angle was born in 1969 and grew up in Niskayuna, a small town in upstate New York. A large General Electric research facility was nearby, and young Angle became fascinated with its intricate machines. As he noted to an interviewer for *Business Week* Online, "I was always more interested in hands-on building than theory."

Angle went to the Massachusetts Institute of Technology (MIT) and received his B.S. in electrical engineering and M.S. in computer science. While studying at MIT, Angle happened to notice the Mobile Robotics Laboratory run by pioneer robotics researcher Rodney Brooks. After they chatted, Brooks hired Angle as a summer helper on the project to build Genghis, an insect-like walking robot.

The opportunity to build or work on a variety of innovative robots was exhilarating. Jeff Sutherland, a computer scientist working nearby, recalled in his "Scrum Log" blog that "[Colin] had his early robots hunting me down in my office" using their infrared sensors. Angle also had the opportunity to work at the Jet Propulsion Laboratory (JPL) in Pasadena, California. Here he helped explore designs for new, smaller, and cheaper planetary exploration rovers. The National Aeronautics and Space Administration (NASA) gave him a special commendation for his development of Tooth, an innovative "microrover."

*Colin Angle helped robotics pioneer Rodney Brooks build planetary rovers. Today, his company iRobot makes robots that clean floors and help the military and law enforcement.* (Photo courtesy of iRobot)

## Teaming Up: Brooks, Angle, and Greiner

In 1990, Rodney Brooks, eager to bring mobile robot technology into the marketplace, joined Colin Angle and fellow MIT researcher Helen Greiner to form a company that eventually became known as iRobot Corporation. (The name is a nod to Isaac Asimov's *I, Robot* collection of robot stories.)

Greiner was born in 1969 in London, though she grew up in Long Island, New York. As a young girl interested in science and mathematics, Greiner was inspired by the original *Star Wars* movie to think about building robots like the friendly and versatile R2D2. (She was disappointed, though, to learn that the robot had a human controller inside.) By the time she was 11, Greiner was writing her own programs on an early personal computer and trying to connect it to control the movements of toys.

Like Angle, Greiner earned a B.S. in mechanical engineering and an M.S. in computer science and studied with Brooks at the MIT Artificial Intelligence (AI) Lab. She had also worked at JPL. According to her MIT faculty adviser, Greiner, unlike some of the more theoretically minded students, was interested in how to turn robotics applications into business opportunities.

*Together with Colin Angle and Rodney Brooks, Helen Greiner founded iRobot Corporation Greiner uses finely honed engineering and business skills to bring new robots to market.* (Photo courtesy of iRobot Corporation)

Greiner's skills in robot design and hands-on engineering served her well as iRobot struggled to bring its first products to market. Although she soon found herself the target of tempting offers from other companies, she was determined to follow through with the vision she shared with Brooks and Angle.

# Baby Doll

Rodney Brooks's robot laboratory at MIT has undertaken a long-term effort to develop robots that can in some sense understand and respond appropriately to human body language, facial expressions, and vocal intonations. At MIT, Brooks had developed a research robot called "IT" by 1995. In 1998, Brooks and Angle decided to create a new kind of baby-doll toy based on IT. It would eventually be called "My Real Baby."

Besides having realistic skin and simulated facial muscles, the robot was able to sense how it was being handled. In addition to being able to move its lips, cheeks, and forehead (allowing it to raise its eyebrows, smile, or grimace, for example), the robot could also perform other behaviors, such as sucking its thumb or a bottle.

The doll's "emotional state" changed according to how it was handled. For example, if held upside down, it became "unhappy" and complained with varying degrees of intensity. The doll would laugh when tickled and burp when patted on the back—though it sort of flinched if approached too quickly from in front. The doll even appeared to "learn" by speaking increasingly complex statements after it had been played with for many hours.

This rather sophisticated behavior required that the doll have a large variety of parts. For example, a ball-bearing in a cage sent signals that the robot could interpret to determine whether it was being gently rocked or roughly handled. Light sensors tried to determine whether the doll was being hugged or tickled. A magnetic sensor reported whether the baby was being given its bottle.

Angle and Brooks believed they had the basic technology in hand, but when they showed the prototype (called BIT for "Baby IT") to toy companies, they were in for a rude awakening. It turned out that the toy industry did not know what to do with this sophisticated robot disguised as a doll. To start with, the typical retail price for "talking dolls" and similar toys was less than the cost of BIT's parts alone. Further, toy industry marketers had no idea how to market a doll that had so many new and hard-to-explain features.

Finally, in 1998, iRobot and Hasbro, one of the world's leading toymakers, made an agreement that iRobot would develop new toy concepts and Hasbro would market those it felt were appropriate.

---

### SOLVING PROBLEMS: DOING ENOUGH WITH LESS

---

With the need to make My Real Baby simpler and cheaper, Brooks and Angle had to modify both its components and its behavior. They had to find ways to fit the software on cheaper processor chips. The five separate motors the prototype had used to control the facial muscles were replaced with a single one that still allowed for the necessary expressions.

As for behavior, the original BIT acted more like a real baby in that it would keep crying until "fed." But since My Real Baby had to meet the more limited attention spans and patience of children, it was modified so that even if not fed, it would eventually get over its hunger and be ready to play again. And instead of having the doll determine whether its diaper had been changed for a new one, they reconfigured the doll to make it satisfied even if the same diaper is removed and put back on—from "virtually wet" to "virtually dry."

These changes highlight the difference between the research robots found in Brooks's MIT lab and the products sold by iRobot. Research robots are designed for exploring interesting concepts and problems in as much depth as possible. But while what is learned in research can be applied to create innovative products, when an inventor becomes an entrepreneur, a different goal must be kept in mind. The customer can be intrigued but must ultimately be satisfied—and at a price he or she is willing to pay.

Another key to iRobot's success may have been the way it has been able to reuse and build upon its technological base. Thus the logic and behavior for a doll could be applied to a robotic pet as well. The behaviors for an automatic vacuum cleaner should be applicable to, for example, an automatic mopper or duster or even a robotic lawn mower. Additional behaviors can be added to account for particular requirements.

---

My Real Baby was the first fruit of this agreement, reaching stores just in time for Christmas 2000.

While sales of My Real Baby were disappointing, the toy was a milestone in robotics. As Rodney Brooks noted to Joseph Pereira of the *Wall Street Journal* Classroom Edition Online, "for the first time our robots [had] to interact with countless thousands of real

people in ordinary homes, not graduate students interested in eso-
teric aspects of human psychology."

In the following years, a number of other companies also decided
that robot toys and "pets," such as Sony's Aibo dog, were the wave
of the future. iRobot and Hasbro responded with a walking dinosaur robot for the 2002 season.

## Household Robots: A Different Approach

As Angle, Greiner, and Brooks looked for new robot applications, one that soon came to mind was building a smarter vacuum
cleaner. While dolls were something of a niche market, virtually
everyone owned a vacuum cleaner and faced the regular, tedious
chore of pushing it around the house in the never-ending battle to
eliminate dust.

The question was how to build a robotic vacuum cleaner that
could do its job virtually unattended. While at MIT, Angle, Greiner,
Brooks and other researchers built generally very complex experimental robots. As Angle told *Robotics Trends,*

> *When I was at MIT, I built a robot that had everything you could
> dream of in a robot, it was small and had 23 motors, 11 computers,
> 150 sensors, everything. It was over the top, but it could never work
> for more than an hour at a time.*
>
> *After I finished it I thought, what's next? I had built the robot
> of my dreams, but I was not satisfied. The answer was that it was
> a research project. It was not a robot that would touch people in
> their daily lives. The visions portrayed in science fiction novels had
> not yet been achieved. I wanted a robot that could clean my house.
> I wanted to do something other than making interesting "one off"
> robots.*

Angle and Greiner learned that it is not easy to turn high-fly-
ing robot ideas into viable products. First, there is the difference
between the design of a research robot and a product that has to
be cheap enough to find a consumer market. As Angle noted to
*Business Week* Online:

*That's [the] big problem with robotics in general: People want to sit down and build robots that cost hundreds of thousands of dollars, and in some cases, that funding has been there. Without worrying*

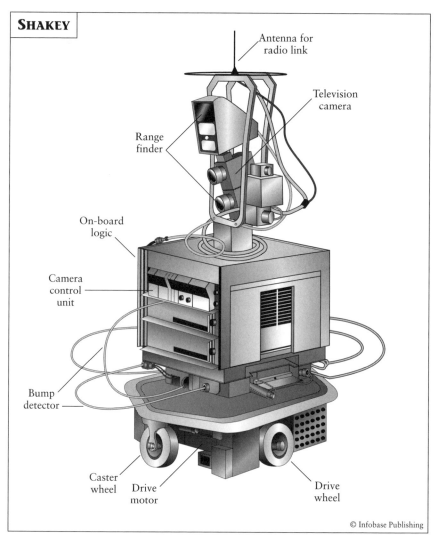

**SHAKEY**

Antenna for radio link

Television camera

Range finder

On-board logic

Camera control unit

Bump detector

Caster wheel

Drive motor

Drive wheel

© Infobase Publishing

*Built around 1960 at the Stanford Research Institute, Shakey was the prototype of a traditional artificial intelligence–based mobile robot. Even though computers are far more powerful today, a simpler approach may be better for creating simple robot appliances.*

*about costs, you can do anything. The challenge is building something for which the final value exceeds the bill of materials.*

Working with Brooks, Angle and Greiner realized that a whole different approach was necessary for making robots a consumer appliance as affordable and accessible as vacuum cleaners, microwaves, or washing machines. Drawing on Brooks's ideas about robots that combine simple behaviors to perform desired functions, they removed nearly all the AI from the equation.

Consider how a typical AI researcher would design a robotic vacuum cleaner. First, the robot would get a complete computer vision system and software to maintain an internal map of each room. The robot would calculate an optimum path to ensure that it missed no spot of dirt on the floor, while identifying obstacles in advance.

To do this, the robot would need cameras (probably with stereoscopic vision) and software that could characterize and locate objects in the room. It would also need some way to keep track of which areas had been cleaned and which were still dirty.

The iRobot team realized that robots with that level of intelligence were complex and hard to make reliable. Indeed, even the most advanced experimental AI robots would have problems dealing with the changing environment of the home. What happens when one of the objects in the robot's internal map is the family cat, which moves between the time of initial calculation and the beginning of the cleaning pass? (It is doubtful the cat will appreciate being vacuumed!)

Assuming they could even build such a robot, it would probably cost about as much as a new car. Not many consumers will pay that kind of price for a humble household appliance.

## Behavioral Building Blocks

The iRobot team decided to take a radically different approach, following Brooks's principle of combining simple behaviors to get effective performance. The robot, called Roomba, follows a random spiral-like path around the room, cleaning as it goes. It has no idea where it is located in the room or where obstacles may be located. When it bumps into something, it reverses itself (using a few special tricks for dealing with corners and such).

Roomba does not know what parts of the room have already been cleaned; however, this is not a problem because its modified random path is designed to make sure it eventually reaches every area. When the machine detects a wall, it follows it while a spinning side brush collects dirt in edges and corners. There are also two counter-rotating brushes that bring larger pieces of debris within range of the vacuum nozzle.

Roomba has an additional feature that helps it clean efficiently. When special sensors near the brushes detect high concentrations of dirt, Roomba switches to a tighter cleaning pattern so it spends more time cleaning in the immediate area. When dirt is no longer detected, the robot reverts to its general wandering. This combination of random navigation and focused cleaning behavior results in a quite satisfactory job—Roomba can clean an average room in about 20 minutes.

*The compact, unthreatening Roomba can quietly keep floors clean and return to its recharging station when necessary.* (Photo courtesy of iRobot Corporation)

Roomba uses infrared beams to detect stairs and other "cliffs." As long as the robot is on a level surface, the beam bounces back to a detector. If the beam does not bounce back, Roomba reverses direction to avoid falling. Finally, the robot can be confined to a particular area by placing a special beacon.

Even with a good design, iRobot's developers also had to master the practical problems of mass-producing consumer products. With a single research robot in a laboratory, it is not a problem to fix glitches or replace parts that are not up to spec. With consumer

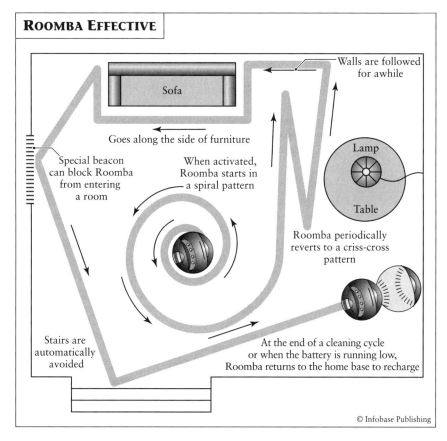

ROOMBA EFFECTIVE

Walls are followed for awhile

Sofa

Goes along the side of furniture

Special beacon can block Roomba from entering a room

When activated, Roomba starts in a spiral pattern

Lamp

Table

Roomba periodically reverts to a criss-cross pattern

Stairs are automatically avoided

At the end of a cleaning cycle or when the battery is running low, Roomba returns to the home base to recharge

© Infobase Publishing

*Roomba's effectiveness comes from its simple design as well as a combination of cleaning routines that provides good floor coverage.*

products, quality control and reliability are paramount, as iRobot found when they had to send out a hundred thousand plug-in adapters to fix a problem with the Roomba's battery-recharging systems.

Fortunately, engineering and marketing seemed to come together in an ideal match with Roomba. By 2005, more than 1.2 million Roombas had been sold, at about $200 each. Later that year, Scooba, a robotic mopper, was introduced.

In its more recent Roomba Discovery model, iRobot made a number of modest improvements to the robot's cleaning, storage, and power-charging systems. But the most interesting advances make Roomba smart enough to change its cleaning pattern according to the size of the room and the amount of dirt it collects, as well as using an infrared beacon to home in on its docking station when a recharge is needed. Other companies, such as Applica and Sharper Image, have come out with competitive cleaning bots. The household robot, at least in specialized form, seems to have won consumer acceptance.

## Robots on the Front Lines

Military and law enforcement agencies are intensely interested in using robots to perform tasks that are difficult or dangerous for humans, such as disarming an improvised explosive device or approaching a suspect in a hostage situation safely. iRobot has developed a machine called the PackBot for these functions.

The PackBot weighs about 50 pounds (23 kg), so it can be easily transported in the trunk of a police car or even carried by its operator. The robot has tracks like a tiny tank, but its rotating flippers enable it to clamber over rubble and even climb stairs. Specialized versions are equipped with different types of sensors, cameras, and attachments for a particular task.

Greiner has noted with pleasure the letters she receives from U.S. soldiers in Iraq and Afghanistan whose lives have been saved by one of the more than 150 Packbots that have helped them search for and disarm explosive devices found in buildings and caves.

In July 2005, iRobot introduced the PackBot Explorer. This model was designed for a variety of surveillance missions. It has three separate cameras and can be fitted with specialized sensors.

## Future Household Robots

Angle and the crew at iRobot believe the future for consumer robots is promising. They believe that while many household tasks are much more complex than vacuuming floors, it should be possible to eventually build robots to do them. As entrepreneurs, their challenge is to identify the time when available technology and an appropriate design can deliver robots whose performance will justify their cost.

Meanwhile, as Angle noted to *Business Week* Online:

*The Roomba is a first step. It's not intimidating. And it works. People find that surprising. The Roomba has gotten more people to accept the idea that robots can be useful. Maybe it could be a home-maintenance system, where your floors are forever clean. Then think about robots taking care of people, especially for elder care. That's ultimately the killer application for robotics.*

In an interview with Engadget.com, Greiner expanded on this vision. She believes that

*in 30 years chores around the house will be a thing of the past. The robots will have evolved from automatic appliances to home automation systems. iRobot (and others) will be selling clean floors, clear windows, organized closets, mowed lawns, sparkling toilets, and dust-free surfaces that the consumer never has to think about. The robots just come out and do the job when it needs to be done.*

*There will be a robot in every squad car and it would be unthinkable to send an officer into an unknown situation. Robots will help the massive problems caused by the world aging demographic. Predictions currently are dire about the availability of caregivers for the folks who will need them. Enter the robots, that allow doctors to go on house calls through telepresence, that bring your grandmother water in order to hydrate, assure medication compliance, and even find the spectacles that Grandpa has lost for the 1000th time.*

In the nearer term, iRobot has a prototype remote-control robot that could allow someone to "phone home" via the Internet and guide the robot around the house (it can even climb stairs). Besides checking to make sure everything is all right, the user can use the robot's communications abilities to chat with family members, perhaps even read a bedtime story to the children.

Although iRobot is now, with more than 200 employees, the world's largest robot maker, Greiner, Angle, and other robotics entrepreneurs will face many tough obstacles in developing new applications. The remote control and telepresence applications (such as military, law enforcement, and home monitoring) are probably easier, since they do not involve having the robot make autonomous high-level decisions. There would be great consumer interest in being able to buy a "Jetson's" robot that is smart and versatile enough to perform many different tasks, but even the most advanced laboratory research robots can perform only limited, well-defined tasks in simplified environments (lawn-mowing robots are already modestly popular). Perhaps we will have to be content with specialized robots for some time to come.

## Honored for Innovation

Angle and Greiner were named New England Entrepreneur of the Year for 2003 by Ernst and Young. Greiner has also been honored as an "Innovator for the Next Century" by MIT's *Technology Review* magazine, as well as receiving the "Demo GOD" award from the prestigious DEMO Conference, a showcase for cutting-edge technology.

No doubt the publicity that Angle and Greiner have garnered (and the sight of Roombas patrolling the floors of millions of homes) is likely to help inspire the upcoming generation of young robot designers. Indeed, by 2005, it was reported that young "robot hackers" were modifying Roombas to serve as platforms for their own robotics projects.

## Chronology

| 1968 | Helen Greiner born in London |
| --- | --- |
| 1969 | Colin Angle born in Niskayuna, New York |

| 1988 | Angle and others in Rodney Brooks's research group develop the Genghis walking robot |
| | Angle graduates from MIT with an undergraduate degree in electrical engineering |
| 1990 | Angle, Greiner, and Brooks cofound a company called Artificial Creatures—the company eventually becomes iRobot Corporation |
| 1991 | Angle receives NASA award for Tooth microrover |
| 1999 | iRobot markets the "My Real Baby" robot baby doll |
| | MIT *Technology Review* dubs Greiner an "Innovator for the Next Century" |
| 2002 | iRobot's first Roomba robotic vacuum cleaner hits the market |
| 2003 | Ernst and Young name Angle and Greiner New England Entrepreneur of the Year |
| | iRobot's PackBots are used in Afghanistan and Iraq |
| 2005 | "Scooba," a robot that can mop floors, is introduced |

# Further Reading

## Books

Brooks, Rodney. *Flesh and Machines: How Robots Will Change Us.* New York: Pantheon Books, 2002.

    Describes Brooks's work and approach to robotics as well as his role with iRobot, Inc.

## Articles

Jewell, Mark. "iRobot Co-Founder's Perseverance Now Pays Off." *Technology Review,* May 31, 2005. Available online. URL: http://www.technologyreview.com/articles/05/05/ap/ap_3053105. asp?p=1. Accessed on September 9, 2005.

    Interview with Helen Greiner giving some personal background as well as discussion of iRobot's products.

Kanellos, Michael. "Invasion of the Robots." CNET News.com March 10, 2004. Available online. URL: http://news.com.com/ Invasion+of+the+robots/2009-1040_3-5171948.html?tag=nl. Accessed on August 15, 2005.
  Describes recent developments in robotics that are being spurred by the availability of cheaper, more powerful processors, sensors, and software.
———. "The Leader of the Robot Pack." CNET News.com, July 7, 2005. Available online. URL: http://news.com.com/The+leader +of+the+robot+pack/2008-1008_3-5776430.html. Accessed on September 7, 2005.
  Interview with Colin Angle.
Pereira, Joseph. "Natural Intelligence: Helen Greiner Thinks Robots Are Ready to Become Part of the Household." *Wall Street Journal* Classroom Edition Online, October 2002. Available online. URL: http://www.wsjclassroomedition.com/archive/02oct/COVR_ ROBOT.htm. Accessed on September 24, 2005.
  Discusses Helen Greiner's work and plans for bringing robots into the home.
"Robots: Today, Roomba. Tomorrow . . ." *Business Week* Online, May 6, 2004. Available online. URL: http://www.businessweek. com/print/technology/content/may2004/tc2004056_2199_tc_168. htm?tc. Accessed on September 8, 2005.
  Interview with Colin Angle discussing the prospects for consumer robotics.
Torrone, Philip. "Interview: Helen Greiner, Chairman and Cofounder of iRobot, Corp." Engadget.com, August 2, 2004. Available online. URL: http://features.engadget.com/entry/8154940951659251. Accessed on January 15, 2006.
  Interview with Greiner talking about iRobot's products and future plans.
"Vendor Spotlight: Do What You Love and Success Will Follow: An Interview with iRobot's Colin Angle." *Robotics Trends,* September 12, 2003. Available online. URL: http://roboticstrends. com/displayarticle95.html. Accessed on July 14, 2005.
  Colin Angle discusses iRobot's consumer and military robots and the robotics industry as a whole.

*Web Sites*

iRobot. URL: http://www.irobot.com. Accessed on August 5, 2005.
Corporate Web site describing iRobot's products and plans.

**Robotics Online.** URL: http://www.roboticsonline.com. Accessed on September 25, 2005.
Sponsored by the Robotics Industry Association, this site includes news and a buyer's guide for robot products.

# 5

# ROBOT EXPLORERS

## DONNA SHIRLEY AND THE MARS ROVERS

In 1997, humankind's first mobile robot planetary explorer bounced across the surface of Mars, astride a lander platform surrounded by giant air bags. Called *Sojourner* and smaller than a child's wagon, the little machine would begin a new era of exploration of our most enigmatic planetary neighbor. Built for less than the cost of a hit Hollywood movie, *Sojourner* represented not only new ideas in robotic space exploration but also a style of creative management much different from the top-down bureaucracy that had troubled the National Aeronautics and Space Administration (NASA) for years.

The manager who guided and helped shape the complex Mars Pathfinder program was Donna Shirley, a woman whose own sojourns in traditionally male-dominated fields continually challenged her perseverance and creativity.

## A Love of Engineering

Donna Shirley was born in the small town of Wynnewood, Oklahoma, in 1941. Because her father was the town doctor and her mother the daughter of a prominent minister, Shirley and her younger sister Margo were closely scrutinized for "proper" behavior. This was a real problem for the young girl. In her autobiography, *Managing Martians*, Shirley recalled that as a child,

*I had a difficult time making friends with the girls anyway because I wasn't interested in dolls, dress up games, or pretending to be a princess. . . . I much preferred to play cowboy or detective, but few of the boys were willing to play those kinds of games with a girl.*

Shirley loved to read books about airplanes and flying adventures, imagining that she was a bush pilot transporting "flying doctors" in the Australian outback. When she was 10, she saw a reference in a graduation ceremony to "aeronautical engineering." When she asked what that meant and was told "building airplanes," she knew that was what she wanted to do.

*Donna Shirley managed many aspects of the program that brought* Sojourner, *humankind's first mobile robot space explorer, to the surface of Mars in 1997.* (Photo courtesy of Donna Shirley)

Shirley also became fascinated by space exploration, particularly as portrayed by science fiction writer Arthur C. Clarke's novel *The Sands of Mars.* Shirley's interest in aerodynamics was visceral as well as intellectual. She was eager to learn to fly, and by age 16, she was ready to go "solo," having learned the feel of flying an Aeronca Champ, a fabric-winged trainer with a tiny 65-horsepower engine.

## Getting Respect

After high school, Shirley attended the University of Oklahoma. Telling her adviser that she wanted to enroll in the engineering program, Shirley recalled in her autobiography the curt response that "Girls can't be engineers." When she was enrolled in engineering courses for which she had not been prepared, Shirley had to struggle to earn a passing grade in her first year. Seeking an alternative that still suited her interest in aviation engineering, she changed majors and graduated in 1963 with a degree in technical writing.

Shirley went to work at McDonnell Aircraft in St. Louis, Missouri, as a specifications writer. There she had her first experience of disdain and even sexual harassment in a virtually all-male workplace. She decided to go back to the University of Oklahoma, where she received her bachelor's degree in aerospace and mechanical engineering in 1965. When she returned to McDonnell Aircraft that year, it was as an aerodynamicist.

In 1966, Shirley visited the Jet Propulsion Laboratory (JPL) in Pasadena, California. This was the research organization that was powering America into the space age with innovative propulsion systems and vehicles. In the late 1960s, Shirley had the opportunity to help design a space probe that would later become *Mars Pathfinder,* while finishing studies leading to a master's degree in aerospace engineering in 1968 from the University of Southern California.

In the early 1970s, Shirley worked as a specialist and then became a manager on the *Mariner 10* project, which would successfully send back the first detailed high-quality pictures of Venus and Mercury. The challenges and rewards of managing complex projects began to appeal to her almost as much as the desire to build innovative machines. Shirley was also designated as the group's media representative, responsible for explaining the exciting but complicated world of space science in terms that ordinary people could understand. The result of her excellence in all of these roles was a NASA Group Achievement Award.

In 1979, Shirley reached project leader status, being placed in charge of the effort to design a mission to Saturn. (This would eventually become the Cassini-Huygens mission, which explored Saturn and its moon Titan starting in 1997). Shirley also worked on projects to design better computer systems for military satellites and to develop a viable space station.

## Designing Space Robots

During this time, Shirley also became interested in robotics and its application to the design of space probes. Space applications impose special requirements on robots. The environment of space is incredibly harsh: Temperatures can change rapidly from hundreds of degrees (in direct sun) to nearly absolute zero in shadow. A constant sleet of charged particles and radiation strikes the spacecraft, and it can be suddenly augmented by solar flares. Here on Earth, the atmosphere protects living things and machines from most of these effects, but materials used in spacecraft and space robots must be specially selected and "hardened" in order to survive in the hostile environment of space.

Space probes must also endure the shock of liftoff from Earth and survive a journey of tens or hundreds of millions of miles. Probes intended to visit the surface of a planet will undergo what will at best be a bumpy landing. Although some redundancy (development of duplicate or backup systems) can be built into the spacecraft design, this can only go so far. Weight is the main constraint: Every additional pound or kilogram means the launching rocket has to be bigger. A related constraint is cost—particularly in the modern era, in which NASA's budget has greatly declined from the triumphant Apollo days of the 1960s.

The engineers on Shirley's team thus had to make hard choices. For example, could they afford the weight and cost of a backup radio transmitter? If the main transmitter failed, having a second one might ensure that the space probe could send back at least a portion of the planned pictures and instrument readings. Or should the money and weight allowance be used instead to improve the landing system (increasing the chances of a safe touchdown) or perhaps to allow a rover to carry an additional scientific instrument?

As an engineer and designer of space probes, Shirley became familiar with the need to make such trade-offs. But as her managerial responsibilities increased, so did the challenge in getting highly opinionated scientists and engineers to work together effectively. Each instrument on a space probe, lander, or rover represents a capability that someone has probably spent years working and planning for. Theoretical scientists generally want the biggest and best instruments possible, seeking always to see or sense farther. Engineers, on the other hand, want the system to be as reliable as possible. They know that unlike laboratory experimenters, they will have no opportunity to try plugging in a different part once the mission is underway.

## CONNECTIONS: WHY AREN'T THEY HERE?

While our space probes go out into the solar system and beyond, should we expect to meet robot spacecraft from other worlds?

Since the mid-1900s, scientists and science fiction writers have speculated about the likelihood and prevalence of intelligent civilizations in the universe. SETI (Search for Extraterrestrial Intelligence) has attempted to detect radio signals from such civilizations, but so far there are no confirmed signs that anyone is out there.

What is the real likelihood that we are not alone in the galaxy? One approach to answering this question, taken by radio astronomer Frank Drake, was to plug probabilities (such as the presence of suitable stars and Earth-like planets) into an equation, which seemed to yield thousands of possible intelligent civilizations in the Milky Way galaxy alone. But this brings up the "Fermi paradox," first suggested by the famous nuclear physicist Enrico Fermi: "If there are so many civilizations out there, why has no one visited us?"

The usual answer is that the distances between stars are so immense that even advanced civilizations would have to consume most of their available resources to send starships to visit even nearby stars. Perhaps civilizations do not last long enough to explore very far—or they do not consider the effort worthwhile.

The possibility of building advanced, self-reproducing robots changes the equation somewhat. If such robots can mine the resources they need, build their own starships, and spread from star system to star system, calculations suggest that such a robot "swarm" should be able to spread through our galaxy in only a few hundred thousand years. Shouldn't humanity already have been visited by space robots?

Of course, there are far too many unknowns for us to be confident about such speculations. Perhaps the robots came and went millions of years ago, after deciding that Earth was not that interesting. Or perhaps there were no robots because such a mechanical civilization would presumably have begun through the efforts of flesh-and-blood roboticists. If paleontologist Peter Ward and astronomer Donald Brownlee's argument in their book *Rare Earth* (2000) is correct, advanced intelligent life may be exceedingly rare. It may be humans who will get to build the robots who ultimately explore the galaxy!

# Missions to Mars

The red planet Mars has had a special place in the human imagination as long as people have looked at the sky. About a century ago, the astronomers Giovanni Schiaparelli and Percival Lowell thought they saw the canals of an advanced civilization on the Martian surface. Science fiction writers such as Arthur Clarke, Ray Bradbury, and Kim Stanley Robinson have portrayed imaginative future histories of human exploration and the colonization of Mars.

As soon as people figured out how to launch spacecraft that could overcome the Earth's gravity, Mars (after the Moon) beckoned to be explored. In the 1960s, many probes from the United States and the Soviet Union failed to reach the red planet (or went silent), until in 1969, when the U.S. *Mariner 6* and *Mariner 7* spacecraft sent the first stunning photos of the Martian landscape back to Earth.

## *Mariner 9*

After earning her master's degree in Aerospace Engineering at the University of California in 1968, Shirley began a new job at JPL, where she would spend most of her career. At first she worked on a team that analyzed the complex trajectories, or paths, that spacecraft must take in order to navigate the solar system. This work is difficult because, unlike cars or even airplanes, spacecraft cannot take more or less direct paths in planning trips from, for example, the Earth to Mars.

A trajectory not only has to be designed to bring spacecraft from one moving planet to another, but it must also account for the gravitational forces of the Sun, Moon, and other planets. Even the pressure of the Sun's light on the craft must be accounted for, because even a small uncorrected acceleration over time can push the craft off course and cause it to miss its target.

Because the amount of fuel is limited, some long-range space missions use the gravity of one planet (such as Venus) to accelerate the craft on its way to another planet (such as Mercury in the case of *Mariner 10*). Since planets are not perfectly round, their gravitational field is also irregular, and the exact angle and area of approach has to be calculated in order for the "slingshot" effect to work properly. In her autobiography, Shirley describes the whole process as being like "trying to thread a needle from 50 million miles away."

Although this work might interest people with a more theoretical and mathematical bent, Shirley soon became bored with planning trajectories for hypothetical missions that were not yet funded. In 1973, Shirley was able to get a job as a mission analyst for the Mariner Venus-Mercury mission. Her first task was to schedule an exact launch date for the mission. For each interplanetary mission, considerations of planetary positions and available fuel dictate a range of time called a "launch window," in which a launch is feasible. Shirley had to then pick a time within the window that would best ensure that the many different experiments to be done by Mariner would be ready for flight. This task led to conflict among the seven principal investigators (the people in charge of the main experiments). For example, researchers involved with photography naturally wanted the craft to pass on the sunlit side of Mercury. On the other hand, people concerned with studying charged particles and magnetic fields wanted to be on the dark side of the planet, where interference from the nearby Sun would be minimized. Shirley's skills at diplomacy and the art of compromise were put to the test!

## Managing Risk

Shirley had to develop her communications skills in reconciling the conflicts over priorities for space missions. Since the only language the different scientists seemed to have in common was mathematics, Shirley devised simple equations that related the different considerations to one another. She then asked the scientists to give numerical "goodness values" to the importance of, for example, certain photographic opportunities. Shirley's innovative conflict resolution approach must have impressed her superiors because she won a promotion to project engineer.

Another aspect of management that interested Shirley was the need to manage risk. Space flight is full of risks, of course, but the attitudes toward risk among the different people involved in a mission vary

## TRENDS: MILESTONES IN NASA's MARS EXPLORATION

Humanity has explored Mars for more than four decades. The following chart summarizes the most significant successful missions.

| Year | Spacecraft | Mission |
|------|------------|---------|
| 1964 | *Mariner 4* | Small space probe sent on long trajectories to Venus, Mars, and Mercury. Collected first close-up photos of Mars |
| 1969 | *Mariner 6* and 7 | Mars flyby missions returned many pictures and atmospheric data |
| 1971 | *Mariner 9* | First probe to orbit Mars rather than just fly past. Photo mosaics had many spectacular features, including giant volcanoes and canyons |
| 1975 | *Viking 1* and 2 | First spacecraft to land successfully on another planet (July 1976). Conducted soil analyses and searched for possible signs of life |
| 1996 | *Pathfinder* | First landing of a rover (*Sojourner*) on Mars (in 1997). Used a new landing method with parachutes and airbags. In addition to taking pictures, the rover visited rocks and performed spectroscopic analyses |
| 2003 | Mars Exploration Rovers | Rovers *Spirit* and *Opportunity* have ranged for unprecedented distances and are continuing to operate more than two years past their design life |
| 2006 | *Mars Reconnaissance Orbiter* | Arriving in March, the orbiter will spend six months adjusting its orbit before beginning science operations |

The history of Mars exploration has also been marked by painful failures. Several Soviet probes failed in the 1960s and early 1970s, as did two of NASA's Mariner missions. Communication was lost with the *Mars Polar Lander* (launched in 1999), while the *Mars Climate Orbiter,* launched in 1998, burned up in the planet's atmosphere. The ambitious Russian *Mars '96* spacecraft mission was also lost.

according to what they are invested in emotionally. The research scientist is often driven by the desire to learn as much as possible from an experiment, even if this might have a negative impact on other aspects of the mission. To the engineers who are responsible for particular components, any risk that puts unnecessary stress on the component is to be avoided.

Even choosing the launch date involved a balancing of risk. If there is a four-week launch window, a launch date two weeks into that period might allow for better final preparation of experiments—but it brings the risk that if something goes wrong there will not be enough time to fix it and still launch within the window.

On November 3, 1973, *Mariner 10* launched successfully. Then, as the craft approached its first rendezvous at Venus the following January, one thing after another began to go wrong. The star tracker that was supposed to keep the star Canopus lined up as a navigation reference instead began to follow the little glowing flecks of paint that were peeling off the spacecraft. The gyros that were supposed to keep the craft stable also began to fail.

As Shirley offered suggestions and helped keep people communicating, the guidance control team had to figure out how to maneuver the spacecraft without turning it and possibly losing control. To make things worse, the main power system went out. On top of all that, the scientists had accidentally vented much of the gas that was supposed to be used for controlling the craft's attitude, or angle.

Finally, the Mariner team came up with a plan. The craft had two big movable solar power panels. They decided to use these panels like sails, using the pressure of the "wind" of photons from the Sun to turn the craft in the required direction. This had to be done very carefully because if the craft turned too fast the automatic attitude control system would fire the jets, wasting the small amount of gas that was left. To control the operation of the spacecraft, extremely precise commands had to be sent to the onboard computer, which could hold fewer bytes of data than are needed to store this paragraph.

Despite these difficulties, *Mariner 10* was a spectacular success, looping around Venus to take pictures and readings. About a month later, the craft passed Mercury in the first of three flybys, getting the first good pictures and data from that tiny sun-seared world.

The mission cost $98 million, the cheapest planetary mission yet attempted. That suggested the possibility of even greater achievements to come.

## Better, Faster, Cheaper

Meanwhile, Mars continued to beckon. The results of the Mariner Mars missions had whetted scientists' appetite for learning more about the planet's geological history and the possible presence of life. In 1976, NASA's two Viking landers became the first space probes to achieve sustained operations on the Martian surface. In addition to the orbiters and their landers taking numerous high-quality photos, the landers obtained and tested soil samples for signs of chemicals that might indicate the presence of life. (The results were inconclusive.)

As impressive as it was, Viking was also both very expensive and limited in its capabilities, since it had no ability to move around the Martian surface. In general, NASA was finding itself in the position of launching only one or two expensive planetary exploration missions each decade or so. With all their eggs in only a few baskets, the failure of a communications or landing system could mean wasting hundreds of millions of dollars and many years of effort. For example, *Mars Observer,* launched in September 1992, was intended to be an ambitious, instrument-filled orbiting laboratory for the study of the Martian climate and geology. In August 1993, however, contact with the spacecraft was lost just as it was scheduled to enter orbit around Mars.

The lack of support for a faltering NASA space exploration program led the agency's new chief administrator, Daniel Goldin, to shake up the bureaucracy. His "better, faster, cheaper" slogan meant that for new space missions, designers would have to be bold and creative in figuring out how to build less expensive, smaller space probes. On the other hand, they would get to launch more often—for Mars, this meant taking advantage of more of the launch windows that arrive every two Earth-years or so.

Shirley had previously worked on a massive one-ton Mars rover design that would have cost about $10 billion to build. Now she was brought back and asked to come up with mini-rovers similar to those some of the more innovative robotics experimenters had been designing—machines small enough to ride along on the "better, faster, cheaper" missions being planned.

## Robots and Rovers

Building a robot that can keep itself out of trouble while navigating through its environment is hard enough. Now put that robot on another planet, where it is not possible to make "service calls." Even sending commands to the robot is more complicated than on Earth, since the radio commands can only travel at the speed of light. In the case of a mission to Mars, the lag between sending and receiving a signal averages about 10 minutes, depending on how far apart Earth and Mars have moved as they follow their respective orbits.

Because of this signal lag, a rover cannot be steered like a remote-control toy car here on Earth. Suppose an obstacle such as a rock

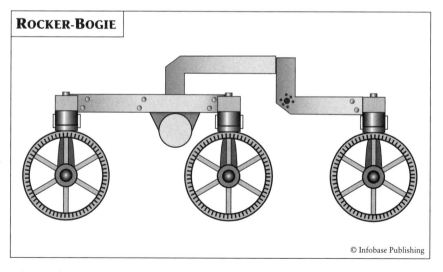

**ROCKER-BOGIE**

*The "rocker bogie" carriage system on the Jet Propulsion Laboratory's Mars rovers allows the wheels to push up and roll over obstacles of considerable size.*

or a pit appears suddenly in the rover's path. It would take at least 10 minutes for that information to reach controllers on Earth and another 10 minutes for a command such as "turn right 30 degrees" to reach the rover. By then the rover may have crashed into something or become hopelessly stuck.

This means that a rover must have considerable autonomy, or the ability to make its own decisions about the environment. With a rover like *Sojourner,* the controllers send detailed instructions for each planned activity, including the location (such as a rock) to which the rover is to move. The robot then takes over, using a camera and laser system to chart a course around obstacles. (This would be greatly aided by an innovative locomotion system featuring wheels that can "rock" or tilt up in order to roll over the smaller obstacles.)

By the 1980s, robotics researchers at JPL and a number of university research labs were developing robots that had some of these navigation capabilities. As computer processors became more powerful and smaller, it began to be possible to put more intelligence aboard a roving robot. Nevertheless, Shirley and the other managers and engineers on the rover team felt they could not adopt the most ambitious ideas of the artificial intelligence researchers. Only an effective partnership between human controllers and the robot would allow for reliable operations on the Martian surface.

Besides navigating and avoiding accidents, software aboard the rover must also include default instructions such as what to do if it loses radio contact with base—in this case the lander, which relays the rover's transmissions to and from Earth, either directly or via satellites in orbit around Mars.

All of the necessary computers, control and communications systems, solar and battery power systems, locomotion systems, and the cameras and science instruments would have to fit in a rover that weighs only 23 pounds (10.5 kg)—less than many dogs!

## *Sojourner's* Truth

Besides her role in planning and organizing the Mars *Pathfinder* mission and rover development, Shirley continued to work with public relations. In one mildly controversial initiative, she organized a

*It is hard to imagine how elated Donna Shirley and her colleagues were when they saw this photo. The lander has arrived, and the cushioning airbags have deflated.* Sojourner *is poised to begin an epic exploration of* Mars. (NASA photo)

contest to name the Mars rover. The winning student's essay offered the name Sojourner, in honor of Sojourner Truth, the American woman who had played an important role in rescuing African Americans from slavery in the mid-19th century. "Sojourner" also means someone who undertakes a long journey, and that would certainly apply to the little Mars rover.

After a journey lasting seven months, *Pathfinder* and its *Sojourner* landed on Mars on July 4, 1997. Or rather, it crashed, bouncing off its air bags 15 times until it finally came to rest almost precisely on the planned target. The elation brought by the first pictures from the lander was matched only by the photos a little later that showed that the rover had been driven down the ramp to plant its wheels firmly on the Martian soil.

As Shirley recounted to interviewer Sally Richards:

*My proudest moment was having my daughter, my second moment was when the* Pathfinder *and* Sojourner *actually worked. When you consider that it was going 17,000 miles an hour and it wasn't supposed to make just another hole in the ground—well, that was a great achievement.*

The adventures of *Sojourner* on Mars attracted unprecedented attention on the Internet, which was becoming an increasingly important outlet for news and outreach. The designers had hoped that the rover would be able to continue its mission for 30 Martian days (called "sols"), but in fact *Sojourner* lasted for 83 Martian days. It was only the failure of the lander's batteries (which had been anticipated) that cut the rover off from being able to relay its

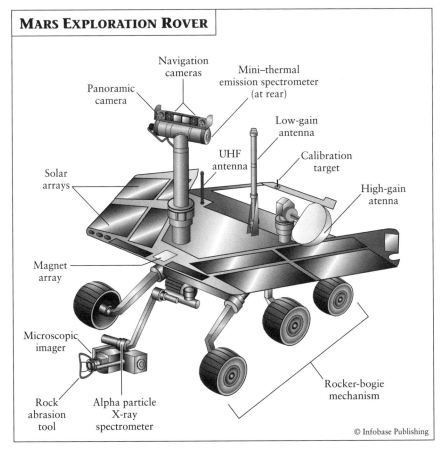

**MARS EXPLORATION ROVER**

Navigation cameras

Mini–thermal emission spectrometer (at rear)

Panoramic camera

Low-gain antenna

UHF antenna

Calibration target

Solar arrays

High-gain atenna

Magnet array

Microscopic imager

Rock abrasion tool

Alpha particle X-ray spectrometer

Rocker-bogie mechanism

© Infobase Publishing

*The current generation of Mars rovers are larger and more capable than* Sojourner, *but they are her true descendents in design and technology.*

---

**ISSUES: SHOULD WE SEND PEOPLE OR ROBOTS TO EXPLORE THE UNIVERSE?**

---

Many critics of the space program argue that human presence in space is a luxury and a waste of resources if we truly want to learn as much as possible about the solar system. While spectacular, the manned Apollo Moon landings did not bring back data that could not have eventually been gathered by robot explorers and sample return missions. The expensive *International Space Station* and the dangerously unreliable space shuttles that served it have returned little scientific benefit. As of 2006, both programs appear to be in trouble and facing an uncertain future.

During those same few decades, robotic explorers have visited every planet in the solar system except Pluto. Landers and rovers have begun an extensive exploration of Mars. Missions such as *Galileo* and *Cassini-Huygens* have probed the giant planets Jupiter and Saturn, landed on the mysterious moon Titan, and even impacted a comet to see what kind of material lay under its surface. (In January 2006, the *Stardust* probe returned a cannister of comet dust to Earth for study.)

When humans travel in space, the bulk of the resources and effort has to go to keeping them alive and healthy. A round-trip journey to Mars would take several years, during which time the astronauts would have to be supplied with food, water, and air and protected from the hard radiation of space. Long-term weightlessness also has

---

communications with Earth. As Shirley noted in her autobiography, *Sojourner* was programmed to keep trying to make contact:

> *On Sol 87 [Sojourner's computer] would have ordered her to start circling the lander, constantly checking, trying to hear a signal. We all had a sad image of the little rover rolling jerkily around the lander like a lost child, calling "Hello? Hello? Is anyone listening?*

In 2004, *Sojourner*'s larger and more gifted children, the rovers *Spirit* and *Opportunity*, landed on Mars. While *Sojourner* had covered a total distance about equal to the length of a football

physiological effects (such as wasting of muscles) that are not fully understood by researchers. Robots do not need air, food, or water. They are much more resistant to radiation, and some space probes have continued to function more than two decades after launch.

Proponents of manned space exploration point out that no robot has the resourcefulness needed to deal with unforeseen emergencies. (This resourcefulness enabled the astronauts in *Apollo 13* to survive their harrowing journey around the Moon.) Robots also lack the broad intelligence and versatility of people. A human geologist on the scene may be able to make better decisions about where and how to explore than a robot and its earthbound controllers.

Advocates of human exploration in space also point out that people identify much more strongly with their fellow humans than with machines, no matter how clever. They argue that support for the space program declined when people stopped doing interesting things in space. Ultimately, only by going to other worlds themselves can humans decide whether they can (or want to) live there.

As of the first decade of the 21st century, the edge seems to belong to the robots. Despite various presidential proclamations, no manned mission to Mars has yet been scheduled. Perhaps as the century progresses our robots will become so sophisticated that they can explore with little direction needed from Earth, while sending back such a broad and rich stream of data that humans can experience other worlds in virtual reality without having to undergo the perilous journey themselves.

field, the new rovers could travel farther than that in a single day. *Spirit* and *Opportunity* were still operating more than two years after their arrival on Mars. Nevertheless, these and future rovers owe much to the engineering and operational knowledge gained by Shirley and her colleagues from *Sojourner.*

## Forging a New Career

Shirley retired from JPL and the Mars program in 1998 and began a new career as a writer and management consultant, drawing upon her decades of experience in managing cutting-edge engineering and science projects. That same year, she published her well-received autobiography, *Managing Martians*. She has also developed an electronic book called *Managing Creativity*. In January 2003, Shirley became director of Seattle's innovative Science Fiction Hall of Fame and Museum.

In addition to receiving two Group Achievement Awards from NASA, Shirley has been honored by groups such as Women in Technology International. She has also been chosen as a Woman of the Year by *Ms.* magazine and received *Glamour* magazine's "Women Who Do and Dare" award. Recognition aside, Shirley believes that what really counts is the number of women who are overcoming obstacles to achieve top-rank careers in engineering and science. In a "chat" on a NASA Web site, she had this advice for young people:

> *The main thing is to be flexible. Usually you don't get to work in the same field your whole career. If you get a sound technical education and are willing to learn and work hard throughout your whole life you'll be O.K. and get to do fun stuff.*

## Chronology

| | |
|---|---|
| **1941** | Donna Shirley born in Wynnewood, Oklahoma |
| **1963** | Shirley graduates from the University of Oklahoma with a degree in technical writing; she works for McDonnell Aircraft in St. Louis |
| **1965** | Having returned to the University of Oklahoma, Shirley earns a B.S. degree in aerospace engineering |
| **1966** | Shirley begins work at the Jet Propulsion Laboratory in Pasadena, California |
| **1968** | Shirley earns a master's degree in aerospace engineering at the University of Southern California |
| **1970** | Shirley becomes the mission analyst for NASA's *Mariner 10* Venus-Mercury expedition |

| | |
|---|---|
| **1973** | *Mariner 10* is launched successfully; Shirley becomes a "project engineer" with management responsibilities, as well as a spokesperson for the program |
| **1974** | Shirley heads a team researching alternative energy sources in the wake of the fuel crisis |
| **1979** | Shirley leads a team that plans what will eventually become the Cassini-Huygens mission to Saturn and Titan |
| **1980s** | Shirley works on research and planning for manned space stations |
| **1987** | Shirley and her team begin designing robotic Mars rovers |
| **Early 1990s** | NASA adopts the "better, faster, cheaper" approach to designing space missions |
| **1992** | Shirley becomes manager of NASA's *Sojourner* rover team |
| **1994** | Shirley becomes manager of JPL's Mars Exploration Project |
| **1997** | The *Sojourner* rover successfully explores Mars in July |
| | Shirley becomes president of Managing Creativity, a consulting and training firm specializing in team-building |
| **1998** | Shirley retires from the Mars Exploration Program and publishes her autobiography, *Managing Martians* |
| **2003** | Shirley becomes director of the Science Fiction Hall of Fame and Museum in Seattle |
| | NASA explores Mars with the *Spirit* and *Opportunity* rovers |

# Further Reading

## Books

Mishkin, Andrew. *Sojourner: An Insider's View of the Mars Pathfinder Mission.* New York: Berkeley Publishing, 2003.
> A vivid account by the project's operations team leader, explaining how the team dealt with myriad technical and management problems.

Shirley, Donna. *Managing Martians.* New York: Broadway Books, 1999.
> Shirley's autobiography, culminating in the success of the *Sojourner* Mars rover mission in 1997.

## Articles

Foust, Jeff. "Seeking a Rationale for Human Space Exploration." *Space Review,* February 9, 2004, n.p. Available online. URL: http://www.thespacereview.com/article/98/1. Accessed on September 11, 2005.
> Discusses the conflicting views of physics professor Robert Park, who favors robotic space exploration, and Robert Zubrin, founder of the Mars Society, who supports human space exploration.

Richards, Sally. "Managing Martians." WITI (Women in Technology International). Available online. URL: http://www.witi.com/wire/feature/dshirley.shtml. Accessed on September 1, 2005.
> Interview with Shirley, talking about her achievements and the challenges for women and girls in science and technology.

Shirley, Donna. "Donna Shirley." NASA Archives. Available online. URL: http://quest.arc.nasa.gov/people/bios/women/dshirl.html. Accessed on September 3, 2005.
> Shirley describes her work during the Mars program in 1996 and gives her philosophy about opportunity and achievement.

## Web Sites

**Managing Creativity.** URL: http://www.managingcreativity.com. Accessed on September 10, 2005.
> The site of Donna Shirley's consulting and training service for developing effective teams that produce innovative products. Includes excerpts from her e-book on the subject.

**NASA's Mars Exploration Program.** URL: http://mars.jpl.nasa.gov. Accessed on August 10, 2005.
> The site describes significant past missions as well as providing updates on current missions and future plans. Includes many interesting images and videos.

**Women in Technology International.** URL: http://www.witi.com. Accessed on September 11, 2005.
> Organization promoting women's careers in scientific and technological professions.

# 6

# THOUGHTFUL ROBOTS

## RODNEY BROOKS AND COG

It was like no robot anyone had ever seen. Most surprising were its big, owl-like eyes that followed visitors' movements. Like a human baby, the robot, called Cog, tried to imitate and learn from what it saw. Also like a baby, it made and responded to vocalizations, although it did not truly understand the words.

Robotics researcher Rodney Brooks is the creator of Cog and other new types of robots. His ideas have found their way into everything from vacuum cleaners to Martian rovers. Today, as head of the Artificial Intelligence Laboratory at the Massachusetts Institute of Technology (MIT), Brooks has extended his exploration of robot behavior into profound realms of philosophy as well as science, asking "What is different about being alive?"

## A Passion for Computers

Rodney Brooks was born in Adelaide, Australia, in 1954. As a boy Brooks was fascinated when he read about computers, but he could only stare through the plateglass window at the city's only visible computer, an IBM mainframe in a downtown office building. Brooks decided to build his own logic circuits from discarded electronics modules from the defense laboratory where his father worked. Eventually, he came up with a machine that could beat anyone at tic-tac-toe—if they accepted the restricted rules necessary to accommodate the machine's limited number of switches.

*Rodney Brooks of MIT has pioneered a new architecture for robots, building in layers of behavior and enabling machines to learn through interaction with humans.* (Photo courtesy of Rodney Brooks)

Brooks also came across a book by Grey Walter, inventor of the "cybernetic tortoise" in the late 1940s. He tried to build his own and came up with "Norman," a robot that could track light sources while avoiding obstacles. In 1968, when young Brooks saw the movie *2001: A Space Odyssey* he was fascinated by the artificial intelligence of its most tragic character, the computer HAL 9000.

Since Australian colleges had not yet established a computer science curriculum, Brooks majored in mathematics at Flinders University in South Australia. He did have access to the university's computer, so he designed a computer language and development system for artificial intelligence (AI) projects. Brooks also explored various AI applications such as theorem-solving, language processing, and games.

## Studying Artificial Intelligence

Brooks was frustrated because there was no formal computer science curriculum in Australia. He then discovered that certain American universities were willing to provide research assistantships—and so he enrolled at Stanford University in Palo Alto, California, in 1977.

Brooks's choice was fortunate because by the 1970s Stanford was becoming one of the world's foremost centers of artificial intelligence research. While working for his Ph.D. in computer science, awarded in 1981, Brooks met John McCarthy, one of the "elder statesmen" of AI in the Stanford Artificial Intelligence Lab (SAIL). He also joined in the innovative projects being conducted by researchers, such as Hans Moravec, who were revamping the rolling robot called the Stanford Cart and teaching it to navigate around obstacles.

In 1984, Brooks moved to the Massachusetts Institute of Technology. Like Stanford, MIT was a burgeoning center of AI research and robotics. There he would undertake more than two decades of innovative research. Much of it would stem from a decision to begin thinking about artificial intelligence in a different way.

## The Challenge of Vision

For his Ph.D. research project, Brooks decided to tackle one of the toughest challenges in AI: creating systems that can identify and "understand" objects in a three-dimensional environment. First, Brooks and his fellow graduate students needed a robot chassis on which to mount the cameras and other gear. Fortunately, a high school student named Grinnell More and two of his friends had started building a simple steerable robot called VECTROBOT. Brooks not only bought one of the machines but also enlisted Moore as an informal research assistant.

They equipped the robot with a ring of sonars (adopted from a camera rangefinder) plus two cameras. The cylindrical robot was about the size of R2D2. Since this was still the 1980s, there were no small computers powerful enough to run the AI software, so the robot was connected by a cable to what was then a powerful minicomputer.

One reason why computer vision is so difficult is because the appearance of an object can change radically depending on the angle from which it is being viewed. A human has no problem knowing, for example, that an upright glass and a glass lying on its end is the same object. Computers, however, have to use complex mathematics to identify objects and their relative positions. These calculations are so intensive that a robot such as Stanford's Shakey, from the 1960s, had to "think" sometimes for hours before being able to move around an obstacle in the room. It took that long to create or update the internal map or representation that the robot needed for successful navigation.

Brooks began to wonder whether the computation-intensive approach to robot vision and navigation was a dead end. After all, as he noted in his talk "The Deep Question":

> *We had a very complex mathematical approach, but that couldn't be what was going on with animals moving their limbs about. Look at an insect, it can fly around and navigate with just a hundred thousand neurons. It can't be doing this with very complex symbolic mathematical computations. There must be something different going on.*

While visiting his wife's family in Thailand, Brooks found himself with a lot of time on his hands. He began to think about how the human brain assimilates the data of the senses. A "classic" AI robot tries to create a "world model" based on the incoming data and then plan and calculate actions.

This could not be how life evolved. The simplest organisms must have developed a way to link quickly, for example, the sensing of a shadow, a vibration, or a rustle to appropriate behavior. The organisms that could make successful connections would survive, reproduce, and pass the genetic blueprint for such neural circuitry on to the next generation.

Brooks realized that as organisms evolved into more complex forms they could not start from scratch each time they added new features. A mouse whose eyes were being completely "rewired" for a sharper image would likely end up inside a cat. Rather, new connections (and ways of processing them) would be added to the existing structure. An eye might thus be able to see motion or contrast better, giving the mouse a better chance of surviving and reproducing.

# A "Brainless" Robot

Brooks decided to rewire his robot (which was now called Allen). Instead of connecting it to a computer that would calculate a map of the environment, he built three "layers" of circuits that would control the machine's behavior. The simplest layer was for avoiding obstacles: If a sonar signal said that something was too close, the robot would change direction to avoid a collision. The next layer generated a random path so the robot could "explore" its surroundings freely. (Of course, if the robot got too close to something, layer 1 would make it shy away.) Finally, the third layer was programmed to identify specified sorts of "interesting" objects. If it found one, the robot would head in that direction.

Each of these layers, or behaviors, was much simpler than the complex calculations and mapping done by a traditional AI robot.

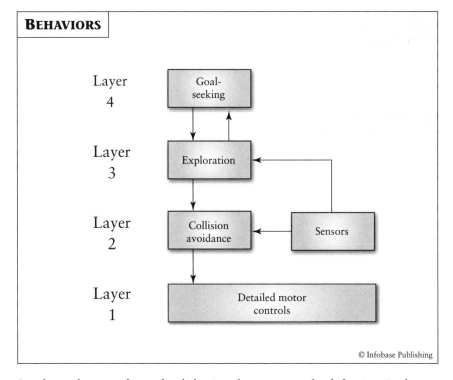

**BEHAVIORS**

Layer 4 — Goal-seeking

Layer 3 — Exploration

Layer 2 — Collision avoidance — Sensors

Layer 1 — Detailed motor controls

© Infobase Publishing

*In a layered approach to robot behavior, the more complex behaviors (such as seeking goals or exploring) are built upon simpler behaviors (such as basic locomotion and avoiding collisions).*

Nevertheless, the layers worked together in interesting ways. The result would be that the robot could explore a room, avoiding both fixed and moving obstacles, and appear to search "purposefully" for things.

In October 1985, Brooks presented his robot to an international robotics research symposium that was attended by many of the world's foremost robot designers. Brooks's robot, Allen, startled observers by its seemingly intelligent navigation and exploration. When they realized that the robot had no "cognition box"—no AI brain in the traditional sense—many researchers in the audience were dismayed. (In *Flesh and Machines*, Brooks recalled learning that two had whispered to each other "Why

## PARALLELS: ARTIFICIAL LIFE AND ARTIFICIAL INTELLIGENCE

The field of artificial intelligence (AI) owes most of its beginnings perhaps to the work of Alan Turing (1912–54), a mathematician and pioneering computer scientist who speculated about the ultimate capabilities of computers while the machines were still in their infancy. In 1950, Turing proposed the famous "Turing Test," which basically suggested that a computer could be considered intelligent if its conversational output could not be distinguished from that of a human under controlled conditions.

In 1956, a seminal conference at Dartmouth College laid out the key problems and objectives of artificial intelligence, raising issues that are still at the heart of the field today. Early approaches such as those by Marvin Minsky (1927– ) and John McCarthy (1927– ) focused on developing artificial reasoning and problem-solving capabilities as well as finding ways to encode knowledge so it could be accessed and used automatically.

An alternative was the "bottom-up" approach that tries to generate sophisticated behavior from simple interactions. The earliest example was the neural network (which was also refined by Minsky), where processing elements are arranged in a network resembling that found in the nervous system of an organism. The system is then given a problem (such as recognizing an image), and those elements that respond correctly are

is this young man throwing away his career?") Scientists who may have spent a lifetime designing and programming robots to act intelligently did not know what to make of a robot whose behavior seemed to emerge mysteriously from simple circuits and subroutines.

In a way, Brooks's robot marked a parting of ways between artificial intelligence and artificial life (AL). AI researchers focused on simulating cognition (reasoning), but AL researchers would concentrate on building layers of sensation and reaction more like that found in the nervous system. Intelligent behavior would not be programmed so much as emerge spontaneously from the interaction of the components.

---

reinforced by giving a higher value. This "trains" the system to perform the task more efficiently. Today neural networks are used in a variety of applications, including image processing, robot navigation, speech recognition, and even credit and security screening.

The field of artificial life (AL) has extended the modeling of natural life processes to mimicking the way organic life reproduces and evolves. An early example was John Conway's Game of Life, a form of "cellular automata" where patterns are manipulated by applying a simple set of rules to each element. Researchers have made interesting applications of this principle, for example, to simulate the behavior of flocks of birds.

The other main thrust of artificial life is genetic programming. Here programs are tested as to how well they can perform a task (such as sorting). This results in a form of natural selection where the successful programs have their code reproduced while the less successful are erased. Like neural networks, genetic algorithms have shown considerable promise in developing applications "from the bottom up."

Most artificial life consists entirely of software simulations inside a computer. However, robotics researchers such as Hans Moravec at the Stanford Artificial Intelligence Laboratory, or SAIL, have built "flocks" of robots that use simple behaviors that, like cellular automation, can result in complex interactions. There has even been some attempt to couple a genetic simulation with a fabrication process to create robots that can "evolve" in form from one generation to the next.

## Robot Insects

By 1988, Brooks and his research group were working on a variety of robots. One, called Herbert, could find and collect empty soda cans, perhaps a useful function for any university setting. Unlike Allen, Herbert had all its computers on board, demonstrating greater autonomy. Further, its ability to control its arm and pick up the cans pointed toward a variety of practical manipulative tasks.

Up to this time, nearly all robots rolled on wheels—none could walk like an animal. Fellow MIT researcher Marc Raibert had demonstrated some walking or hopping robots, but Brooks looked for a different approach to creating a more robust sort of legged locomotion. While watching videos of insects walking over rough terrain, Brooks noticed that they seemed to stumble when missing their footing, but then recovered quickly.

Working with Grinnell More and a new researcher, Colin Angle, Brooks began to build an insect-like robot called Genghis. In *Flesh and Machines,* Brooks said that

> to this day Genghis has been my most satisfying robot. It was an artificial creature. It looked like a six-legged insect. A big *six-legged insect.* . . . As soon as its beady array of six [infrared] sensors caught sight of something, it was off. As long as it could track its prey it kept going, ruthlessly scrambling over anything in its path, solely directed toward its goal. . . . It had a wasplike personality, mindless determination.

Unlike Allen's three layers of behavior, Genghis had 51 separate, simultaneously running computer programs. These programs, called "augmented finite state machines," each kept track of a particular state or condition, such as the position of one of the six legs. It is the interaction of these small programs that creates the robot's ability to scramble around while keeping its balance. Finally, three special programs looked for signals from the infrared sensors, locked onto any source found, and walked in its direction.

Each program was constantly sending or receiving signals (data values) from one or more other programs. For example, the program that read the sensor signals sent a signal to the "prowl" program if a target was detected. The sensor program also sent data to a program that would continuously correct the robot's path, steering toward the target.

Brooks refers to robots like Genghis as being *situated* and *embodied*. A situated robot responds directly to sensory input. Its behavior is shaped by response and interaction, not some abstract model of the world. An embodied robot is just that—in a body that in some sense experiences the world.

As Brooks and his crew began to build more robots that "embodied" these concepts, he had a conversation in 1992 with *Apollo 15* commander David Scott that inspired Brooks to begin exploring ideas for roving robots for planetary exploration. Following the "glory days" of Project Apollo and such probes as *Viking* and *Galileo,* putting mobile robots onto the surface of Mars or other planets seemed to offer an exciting (and perhaps affordable) way to take space exploration to a new level.

Brooks's new layered architecture for embodied robots offered new possibilities for autonomous robot explorers. Brooks's 1989 paper, "Fast, Cheap, and Out of Control: A Robot Invasion of the Solar System," envisaged flocks of tiny robot rovers spreading across the Martian surface, exploring areas too risky to venture into with only one or two very expensive robots. Colin Angle soon built *Tooth,* a 1.1-pound (0.5-kg) microrover. Although the Jet Propulsion Laboratory did not use Brooks's rovers, the *Sojourner* rover that explored Mars in 1997 used wheels similar to those in *Tooth* and had autonomous functions at least partly inspired by Brooks's layered behavior architecture.

## Humanoid Robots

In 1992, about 25 years after the movie *2001: A Space Odyssey* was released, Brooks was thinking about HAL 9000, the humanlike intelligent computer featured in the story. According to the movie, HAL was "born" in a laboratory sometime in the 1990s. In the real 1990s, though, computers and robots still seemed to be decades away from HAL-like behavior.

Having worked with robotic insects, rovers, and other mobile robots, Brooks decided to create a robot that might be able to interact with objects and people in a more humanlike way. Drawing on his experience, Brooks approached intelligence, not by focusing on a brain with sophisticated cognitive programming, but by considering how intelligence actually arises in humans.

As Brooks noted in *Flesh and Machines,* "We humans are not just products of our genes. We are also products of our social upbringing and our interactions with the world of objects. Our culture, too, is a product of our embodiment within the world." This suggested that a humanlike robot should in at least some way look like humans and be equipped with eyes and arms that are similar to ours.

Researcher Hirokazu Kato of Waseda University in Japan had already taken some steps toward creating a humanoid robot. His Wabot-1, built in 1973, could walk on two legs and grasp objects with its hands, as well as "converse" with people in a limited way. Its 1984 successor, Wabot-2, sat at an organ, where it could read music, play the appropriate keys, and push the pedals with its feet. (This sort of research would culminate in the remarkably lifelike P2, P3, and Asimo robots unveiled by Honda starting in 1998.)

Although these robots were humanoid and could even act in humanlike ways, they did not fully satisfy Brooks's need for a situated or embodied robot. Their behavior was essentially controlled by a top-down central program. Harking back to Genghis and its insect-like kin, Brooks wanted to use the behavior-based, layered approach.

Brooks began with the eyes. Unlike a digital camera, the human eye does not have uniform resolution and color vision across its field of vision. The eye has a much wider panoramic view than most cameras (up to about 160 degrees horizontally), but it has much higher resolution and color sensitivity near its center, a place called the fovea. When the eye sees something interesting off to the side (for example, a running animal), it moves quickly or "saccades" to center the vision on that spot. During this time, a human is actually blind, though the brain creates an apparently seamless picture.

Further research suggests that unlike the AI robot, with its internal map of the world, humans are constantly scanning, reacting, and rescanning—programmed by evolution to pay attention to the things that are responsible for physical survival and social success. Thus, the main clue that someone is paying attention to another person is whether they maintain eye contact. Even an infant can tell whether its parent is looking at it. At an age of about nine months, a baby knows when the parent is looking at something else. Gradually, the child learns how to track from the parent's eyes to the distant object.

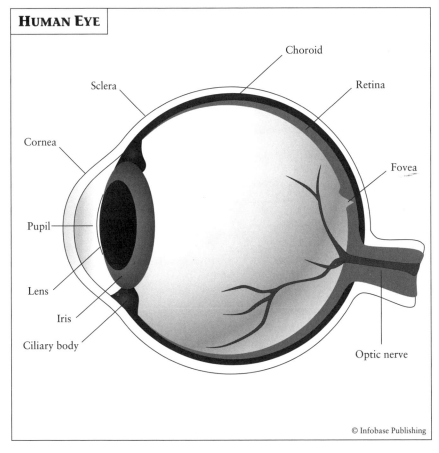

**HUMAN EYE**

Choroid

Sclera

Retina

Cornea

Fovea

Pupil

Lens

Iris

Ciliary body

Optic nerve

© Infobase Publishing

*In the human eye, the concentration of nerves (and thus of image processing power) is at the fovea, the center of the field of vision.*

## Cog

In the early 1990s, Brooks and his colleagues began designing a robot that would embody human eye movement and other behaviors. The robot would be called Cog, short for "cognition," or thought. (There is a touch of irony in this name because Brooks was not emphasizing AI cognition in the usual sense.) Each of Cog's two eyes had separate wide-angle and narrow-angle cameras that mimicked the human eyes' central foveae. Cog's eyes were mounted on gimbals so they could easily turn to track objects, aided by the movement of the robot's head and neck (it had no legs). Cog also had "ears"—microphones that can help it find the source of a sound.

In "The Deep Question," Brooks recalled that as he watched Cog interact with researchers and other visitors to the lab, he was surprised at how humans reacted to their robotic mimic:

> . . . the system with very little content inside it, seems eerily human to people. We get its vision system running, with its eyes and its

*Rodney Brooks is shown here with Cog, a robot that could see and "pay attention" in humanlike ways.* (Photo ©MIT Artificial Intelligence Laboratory, courtesy of Rodney Brooks)

*head moving, and it hears a sound and it saccades to that, and then the head moves to follow the eyes to get them back into roughly the center of their range of motion. When it does that, people feel it has a human presence. Even to the graduate students who designed the thing, and know that there's nothing in there, it feels eerily human.*

As an example of how Cog could engage human attention, film-maker Sanjida O'Connell wrote in the *London Times* that the researchers

*wanted to show that Cog was not programmed to behave in a set manner. So we threw a sixth birthday party for the robot with cake and champagne, and filmed Cog watching its guests. Cog, although only a torso, is humanoid—it has arms with touch sensors on its fingers, it can hear and see, and it is attracted by movement. It is also being taught to copy: for instance, a student will sort a pile of coloured bricks, with the idea that Cog will watch and learn.*

*One memorable moment was at the birthday party. A baby reached out to Cog and the two, robot and baby, interacted. The baby treated the robot as if it was a person. Cog appeared to be fascinated by the baby but is, as yet, unable to speak or to show emotion.*

The work with Cog continued in the late 1990s with the development of Kismet, a robot that included dynamically changing "emotions." Brooks's student Cynthia Breazeal would build her own research career on Kismet and what she calls "sociable robots."

## Practical Robotics

By 1990, Brooks wanted to apply his idea of behavior-based robotics to building marketable robots that could perform basic but useful tasks. Enlisting two of his most innovative and hardworking students, Colin Angle and Helen Greiner, Brooks founded what became iRobot Corporation. As the new millennium dawned, the company was marketing products such as a highly interactive baby doll, the Roomba robotic vacuum cleaner, and tracked robots for use in the military and law enforcement.

Meanwhile, at MIT, Brooks and the AI Lab are working on Project Oxygen, an effort to make computers pervasive and responsive. Examples include voice control, screens that are also walls of rooms, and the seamless connection of telephone and Web services. The ultimate goal is to have all the power of computers available at a word or a touch wherever people are and whatever they are doing, alone or together.

## What Distinguishes Life?

Brooks has not abandoned his quest to use robots to help humans understand how they came to be intelligent. Nevertheless, he has expressed dissatisfaction with the common attempts to apply computation theory to the understanding of biology. It is not that he is seeking some mystical "vital essence," but rather, as he said in the article "The Deep Question":

> We need a conceptual framework that gives us a different way of thinking about the stuff that's there. . . . We see the biological systems, we see how they operate, but we don't have the right explanatory modes to explain what's going on and therefore we can't reproduce all these sorts of biological processes. That to me right now is the deep question. The bad news is that it may not have an answer.

Despite the remarkable achievements of robots such as Brooks's Cog and the work of his innovative student Cynthia Breazeal with the "empathic" robot Kismet, there is still an intuitively recognized difference between robots and animals (including people). In his *Nature* article "The Relationship between Matter and Life," Brooks compared the efforts of two related fields. Artificial intelligence has focused on modeling perception, cognition, and behavior. On the other hand, artificial life has concentrated on creating simple entities that simulate reproduction, selection, and evolution. Both fields have been successfully used in creating the advanced computer applications we use today.

In the article, Brooks asked why neither AI nor AL has yet succeeded in creating something that the average person would consider to be a living thing. In the early days of AI, it was easy to suggest that computers were simply not powerful enough to do the necessary calculations—and might never be. On the other hand, the well-accepted observation known as Moore's Law states that computer power doubles every 18 months to two years. This has held true: Brooks pointed out that the 1965 chess program MacHack could process only a few thousand game positions a second, while the Deep Blue program that defeated world champion Garry Kasparov in 1997 could churn through 200 million moves in that same time.

This raw power has fueled important advances, including vision systems that can much more quickly identify and analyze features in the environment, as with automatically driven vehicles on Earth and rovers on Mars.

In recent years, Brooks has turned his attention to what researchers have been unable to accomplish, despite ever-increasing computational power. The complex way in which the many "layers" of functioning that comprise living behavior emerge from molecular structures and processes has continued to resist modeling. In his *Nature* article, Brooks suggested several possibilities:

*(1) We might be just getting a few parameters wrong; (2) we might be building models that are below some complexity threshold; (3) perhaps there is still a lack of computing power; and (4) we might be missing something fundamental and currently unimagined in our models of biology.*

Brooks has not given up on the quest. He is trying to identify what the "hard" parts of biology—those that do not fit mathematical models very well—might have in common. He is also looking at "distributed systems" where many cooperating systems work together to form a functional whole. This idea has become very important in the design of computer-operating systems and networks. It is also, after all, the way living organisms work—many specialized cells forming organs and systems that together make a complex life-form.

Meanwhile, Brooks has an assured place as one of the key innovators in modern robotics research. He is a founding fellow of the American Association for Artificial Intelligence and a fellow of the American Association for the Advancement of Science. He has participated in numerous distinguished lecture series and has served as an editor for many important journals in the field, including the *International Journal of Computer Vision.* Besides being an articulate spokesperson for the possibilities of advanced robots changing human perception and society, Brooks has even portrayed himself in a movie directed by Errol Morris and titled *Fast, Cheap, and Out of Control,* named for one of his scientific papers.

## Chronology

| | |
|---|---|
| **1954** | Rodney Brooks born in Adelaide, Australia |
| **1966** | Brooks builds a machine that can play tic-tac-toe |
| **1968** | Brooks is inspired by the HAL 9000 computer from the movie *2001: A Space Odyssey* |
| **1975** | Brooks earns master's degree in pure mathematics from Flinders University of South Australia |
| **1977** | Brooks goes to Stanford University to study computer science and artificial intelligence |
| **1981** | Brooks receives Ph.D. in computer science from Stanford University |
| **1984** | Brooks joins the faculty at MIT and works on robot vision and navigation |
| **1985** | Brooks demonstrates a "behavior-based" robot at an international conference |
| **1988** | Brooks and his group begin to design walking robots |
| **1990** | Brooks founds iRobot Corporation with Colin Angle and Helen Greiner |

| 1992 | Brooks and his colleagues begin working on a new design for planetary rovers |
|---|---|
| **Mid-1990s** | Brooks develops the interactive learning robot Cog, who is followed by Cynthia Breazeal's "emotional" robot Kismet |
| **2003** | Brooks becomes head of the new Computer Science and Artificial Intelligence Laboratory at MIT |

## Further Reading

### Books

Brooks, Rodney. *Cambrian Intelligence: The Early History of the New AI.* Cambridge, Mass.: MIT Press, 1999.
> A collection of Brooks's early papers describing the development of his approach to robotic design; includes both technical detail and wide-ranging philosophical speculation.

————. *Flesh and Machines: How Robots Will Change Us.* New York: Pantheon Books, 2002.
> Brooks gives a vivid account of his research into computer vision and creating robots with humanlike behavior, as well as his speculation about the possible nature of living processes.

### Articles

Brockman, John. "Beyond Computation: A Talk with Rodney Brooks." *Edge,* 2000. URL: http://www.edge.org/3rd_culture/ brooks_beyond/beyond_index.html. Accessed on September 1, 2005.
> Transcript of video interview with Rodney Brooks in which he discusses the limitations of computation and traditional artificial intelligence for understanding living processes.

————. "The Deep Question: A Talk with Rodney Brooks." *Edge* 29 (November 19, 1997). Available online. URL: http://www.edge. org/documents/archive/edge29.html. Accessed on September 9, 2005.
> Transcript of video interview in which Brooks discusses the relationship between biological and digital reality and the possible unknown aspect that makes living things different from our machines.

Brooks, Rodney. "The Relationship between Matter and Life." *Nature* 409 (January 18, 2001): 409–411. Available online. URL: http://people.csail.mit.edu/brooks/papers/nature.pdf.
> Both living things and computational machines are ultimately built from nonliving matter. Brooks explores the possible reasons why living things behave differently from computers and robots.

O'Connell, Sanjida. "Cog—Is It More Than a Machine?" *London Times,* May 6, 2002, p. 10.
> Describes encounters with Cog and discusses Brooks's projects and thoughts about the future evolution and uses of robots.

Sebastian, Tim. "Robot Risk 'Is Worth It.' " BBC News *Hardtalk,* August 19, 2002. Available online. URL: http://news.bbc.co.uk/2/hi/programmes/hardtalk/2202825.stm. Accessed on September 1, 2005.
> Transcript of radio interview with Rodney Brooks, who discusses the imperative to explore human nature through robots, the possible risks, and the question of whether robots can actually feel emotions.

## Web Site

**Computer Science and Artificial Intelligence Laboratory (CSAIL).** URL: http://www.csail.mit.edu. Accessed on October 3, 2005.
> Founded in 2003 and directed by Rodney Brooks, this is an interdisciplinary laboratory drawing from computer and cognitive science, bioengineering, and other disciplines.

# 7

# ROBOT AMBASSADOR

## MASATO HIROSE AND ASIMO

For about two decades, walking robots have strut their stuff in laboratories, with varying degrees of success. More practical service robots have rolled through hospital corridors or vacuumed floors. What if there could be a small, versatile humanoid robot that could not only walk gracefully but also climb stairs with ease? Such a robot could combine practicality with the ability to truly fit into peoples' daily activities. In recent years, the answer to this quest for more versatile robots has begun to emerge. Masato Hirose and his fellow researchers at Honda Corporation have been astonishing and intriguing the world with a succession of such robots, culminating in one called Asimo.

## From Motorcycles to Robotics

Masato Hirose was born on February 7, 1956, in Tochigi Prefecture, Japan. In 1980, he received a degree in precision engineering from Utsunomiya University. After further studies, he went to work for Honda Corporation. In 1986, Hirose was assigned to an innovative robotics project. Although he had no real prior experience in robotics, Hirose, whose childhood had been filled with cartoon superheroes such as "The Mighty Atom" was intrigued with the possibility of bringing science fiction ideas to reality.

Although such an interest in robotics might seem surprising for a company better known for motorcycles and automobiles, Hirose

*Honda chief engineer Masato Hirose astonished the robotics world by unveiling Asimo, a humanoid robot that could mingle with people in everyday situations.*

soon learned that Honda thought of itself not as a car company but as a "mobility company." Honda was potentially interested in anything that could move and do something useful. Although the company (like so many of its Japanese competitors) uses industrial robots on the assembly line, this new effort would be devoted to developing mobile robots that could go anywhere people needed them. In return, what Honda could learn about advanced control systems from robotics research would also help it develop "smarter" vehicles to gain an advantage in the highly competitive auto industry.

## Learning to Walk

Working at the Honda's new Wako Research Center outside Tokyo, Hirose and his four-person engineering team began with a relatively simple project: a walking robot that could carry materials from one part of a factory to another. They started by going to the zoo and observing how animals such as an ostrich walked. They also worked with a person who had two artificial legs, observing how he was able to hike and climb mountains.

Gradually, the researchers were able to identify the key aspects of walking in general and human locomotion in particular, including the range of movement for each joint under different conditions, such as walking on flat ground or climbing stairs. They also designed sensors that could provide the robot with the same sort of information that humans perceive while they are walking. This includes the inner ear's ability to judge speed and changing orientation, as well as the sensing of joint angles and pressure on the foot.

The data entering the robot as it moved was processed by three interacting control systems. The floor reaction control dealt with the impact and rebound of the soles of the feet on the floor and the need to compensate for any unevenness in the surface. The target ZMP control calculated the "zero momentum point"—the place where there is no inertia, taking into account the Earth's gravity

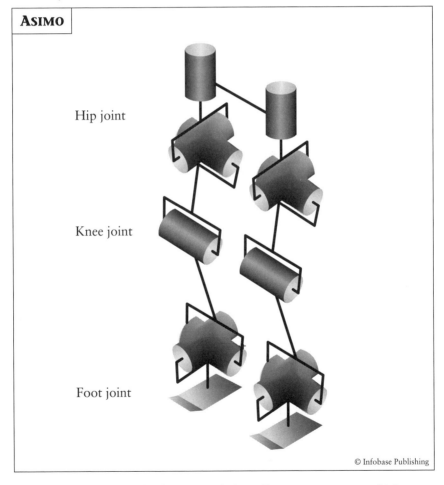

*In Asimo-type humanoid robots a simple but effective arrangement of joints corresponds to the human foot, knee, and hip.*

and the acceleration and deceleration from walking. As long as the ZMP remained within the area supported by the feet, the robot could, if necessary, like a human walker, apply appropriate forces to regain balance if it lost its footing. Finally, the foot-planting location control "shuffled" the feet when necessary to bring the torso into alignment.

## Asimo Debuts

During the next decade, Hirose and his groups created a succession of prototype walking robots. The first of them, P1, which appeared in 1994, is believed by Honda to be the world's first true humanoid walking robot. The next year they demonstrated P2, which dispensed

*Who would have thought that a robot could dance with such fluidity and assurance?* (Photo courtesy of Honda Motor Corp., Japan)

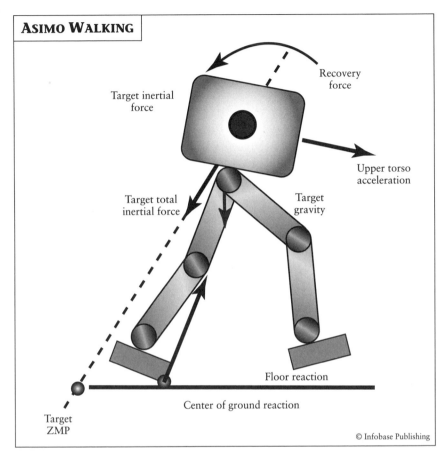

**ASIMO WALKING**

Recovery force

Target inertial force

Upper torso acceleration

Target total inertial force

Target gravity

Floor reaction

Center of ground reaction

Target ZMP

© Infobase Publishing

*Asimo's method of walking involve balancing momentum and taking inertia, acceleration, and "rebounding" from the floor into account.*

with cables and carried all of its computing power on board. This rather hulking robot porter was 72 inches (1.82 m) tall and weighed a hefty 460 pounds (209 kg). P2 demonstrated the potential utility of walking robots for performing useful tasks, but it was rather clumsy and sometimes stumbled and came to a halt. Because of this, Honda released videos to the media, but did not present live demonstrations. In 1997, Honda showed the smaller, more agile P3.

These prototype robots generated some interest in the robotics community, but they were just a prelude to the unveiling of a robot called Asimo in 2000. Although this name evokes famed science fiction writer Isaac Asimov and his robots, Honda insisted that "Asimo" stands for Advanced Step in Innovative Mobility. The robot was about 47 inches (1.2 m) tall and weighed 114 pounds (52 kg).

Asimo's motion was very fluid. Although various forms of robotic walking had been demonstrated by researchers such as Marc Raibert, Hirose and the other Honda engineers wanted their robot to be able to walk in a crowded human environment. To do so, they decided the robot had to walk like a person, with its balancing point on the soles of its feet. They concentrated on smooth movement and the ability to change direction quickly without stopping or losing balance. The Honda researchers developed a feature called "i-Walk," which includes the ability to predict the

---

## OTHER SCIENTISTS: SONY'S ROBOT RESEARCHERS

Sony is the other major Japanese corporation that has gone into mobile robotics in a big way in recent years. While Honda has focused on developing service robots, Sony has concentrated on designing robots for entertainment.

Unlike Honda's Asimo, Sony's robots have already walked their way into thousands of homes. The Aibo robotic dog, introduced in 1999, can walk, recognize and interact with objects, and respond to spoken commands. It even includes a simulated learning process where it can add new commands or behaviors to its repertoire. (Technically minded owners can also use a special programming language, and students can even use Aibo as a handy platform for artificial intelligence projects.) The latest version of Aibo can take pictures and post them on the Internet—making it the first robotic dog to have its own blog!

Sony has also been working on QRIO (short for Quest for cuRIOsity), a humanoid robot that will attempt to blend Asimo-like walking skills with artificial intelligence and playful behaviors. More compact and agile than Asimo, QRIO uses a new type of joint actuator. Like Asimo, QRIO walks dynamically, based on precise positioning of the zero movement point (ZMP)—the point where the forces of gravity

next required movement and shift the center of gravity (and thus balance) at the appropriate time. Another result of this technology is that the robot could change its pace and gait (such as from walking to running) seamlessly.

Researchers such as Honda's Satoshi Shigami have also pointed out that working on a humanoid robot like Asimo can be a profound learning experience. The challenge of creating humanlike robot behavior often surprises the researcher with reminders of just how complex and incredible humans are. Masato Hirose, on a Honda internal video about Asimo, notes that Asimo had something that made him smile ". . . a little bit like the feeling a parent might have."

The latest version of Asimo is a bit taller and heavier. It now includes posture control, a faculty that improves the robot's ability to bend and twist without losing balance, and can even run, albeit at a pace of less than 1.86 miles (3 km) an hour.

and inertia acting on the robot intersect with the ground. If the robot happens to fall, it knows how to "take" the fall in a way that minimizes damage, sticking out its arms and relaxing its "muscles."

For sophisticated interaction with people, QRIO is equipped with face and voice recognition so it can remember particular individuals. The robot also has natural language abilities and can remember information about a person for use in future conversations with that individual. Finally, QRIO has an emotional model. Unlike Asimov's robots, it can occasionally refuse a command simply because it does not wish to comply. A work in progress, Sony's QRIO prototypes are designated SDR (Sony's Dream Robot).

As reported by Yoshiko Hara in *Electronic Engineering Times* in 2002, Sony executive Toshinobu Doi believes that "robots [today] are at the equivalent of the pre-Cambrian era in biology." In the fossil record, there is the "Cambrian explosion"—a relatively brief interval in which the basic plans for multicellular creatures emerged suddenly. In coming decades, if there is to be an explosion in robotic forms and functions, Japan remains a good candidate for the setting. Hara quotes Osaka University professor Minoru Asada as believing that "Japan will be the first society where robots and humans live together." In this sense, Japan will function as a test bed for what happens when robots encounter humans.

Another feature, autonomous continuous movement, allows the robot to plot a new course around a suddenly appearing obstacle without breaking stride. Asimo's improved visual and force-feedback sensors include wrists that can shake hands. If someone pulls or pushes while holding the robot's hand, it will step forward or backward as necessary. Finally, the robot can now run for an hour on its batteries, up from 30 minutes.

## Robotic Ambassador

On New Year's Eve 2001, an Asimo robot joined the Japanese pop group Smap in an onstage dance during a television performance. Masato Hirose was a bit anxious at first about having one of his robots in such a complex, fast-moving environment. As Hirose noted to a reporter for *Asiaweek:*

> *I watched anxiously from under the stage. Anything could have happened—40 people were dancing. Someone could touch Asimo by mistake or their costumes snag him. He mightn't endure the vibrations. I was so relieved when it went well.*

Another triumph for Honda and Asimo came on February 14, 2002, the 25th anniversary of Honda's listing on the New York Stock Exchange. Traditionally, celebrities or other people of symbolic importance are invited to ring the exchange's opening bell from the balcony above the trading floor. This time, though, the bell was rung by an Asimo robot. Soon a total of seven Asimos were traveling around the world to publicize Honda's robotics research. Honda may soon see some tangible returns from its investment in robotics research. The company has announced that in 2006 some of its 40 Asimos will serve as receptionists in Honda offices, where the robot can greet visitors and even serve coffee from a tray. Other Asimos will be offered for lease to companies in Japan and abroad as receptionists, museum guides, and similar roles, at a fee of about 20 million yen ($166,000) a year.

Asimo's greatest benefit for Honda in the coming years is likely to be in the way it has boosted the company's image and served as a recruiting tool. Millions of television viewers in Japan and around the world are coming to associate Honda with not only cars but also nimble, even cute, robotic emissaries of the future. The company also has reported that many graduate engineers have cited Asimo as a reason why they would like to work for Honda.

## Future Helpers

Honda's development of Asimo illustrates the orientation of many Japanese companies to long-term research and development. Currently, the practical uses for an Asimo robot are limited. Hirose acknowledges freely that it may be many years before Honda's robotics research will contribute substantially to the company's bottom line.

Nevertheless, Hirose believes that there will eventually be considerable demand for robots in settings such as hospitals, assisted living centers, and even homes. Hirose suggested to *Asiaweek* that a future descendant of Asimo will be "As you like him to be—your friendly, helpful worker. I'd like it to move and lift things, get them to you, freeing people from some chores." A decade or more in the future, Hirose believes that the helper robots will be able to understand a wide range of instructions in ordinary language. Even though there are no plans to give Asimo a human face and humanlike expressions, people may form attachments to the robots not unlike the bond formed between a person and a guide or helper dog today.

## Other Approaches

In addition to corporations such as Honda and Sony, university researchers have also been taking new robotic "steps." For example, researchers at Cornell University, Massachusetts Institute of Technology, and the Delft University of Technology in the Netherlands are working together on a new approach to robot walkers that promises to make them more efficient.

When a human or animal walks downhill, a burst of energy is used only for the initial push of the leg against the ground, with momentum and gravity doing the rest. Robots such as Asimo must apply additional power in order to control precisely where the step lands.

## Issues: Robots and Religion

When Honda announced its P2 walking robot in October 1995, Hiroyuki Yoshino, the company's president, was worried that some religious groups might consider it blasphemous for people to create humanlike robots. He sent two company officials to the Vatican to ask for an opinion about the robot project.

Fortunately for Honda, the Rev. Joseph Pittau, rector of the Pontifical Gregorian University, was not concerned. He showed the Honda representatives a picture of the famous Michelangelo mural showing God's creation of Adam, with the finger of God touching that of the man made in his image. He explained that just as God put the spark of life into man, he also gave humans the imagination to create things such as robots. As long as the robots were used for constructive purposes, the Vatican stated it would have no objection to them.

In her provocative book *God in the Machine,* Anne Foerst, who is both an MIT robotics researcher and a theologian, explored the relationship between robots, humanity, and God. She placed modern robotics research within a long line of human exploration, including the interplay between myth and science, stories and explanations. Looking at the Jewish tradition of the golem (an artificial human that is motivated by instructions on a special scroll), Foerst suggested that when God created humans in his image, that image included the creative impulse itself. In other words, creation is a "recursive function," and in creating robots and other technology, people are continuing a chain of calls to create what may someday result in our creating true machine partners.

While celebrating the creativity of artificial intelligence (AI) researchers, Foerst warned in her book that "If we see the enterprise of developing artificial intelligence as purely scientific and ignore all the mystical and emotional elements, we will be in danger of falling into the trap of hubris [excessive pride]." Foerst therefore urged that theologians, philosophers, artists, poets, and many others bring their perspectives to understanding the implications of the technology of robotics and AI.

During part of the step, the robot's motors may be actually pushing back against the leg to slow it down to the desired speed.

The researchers at the three universities studied this downhill motion and realized that the same general stroke could be used for walking uphill or on level ground. An initial push from a motor (directly or indirectly) substitutes for the energy that comes from gravity on a downhill walk. The result is a surprisingly simple way to simulate a humanlike gait. It is estimated that this way of walking would use only about a tenth as much energy as Asimo. With battery capacity being such an important factor in the design of mobile robots, this could be a big "win."

Wherever the next steps of a new generation of humanoid robots take them, Masato Hirose and his Honda team have shown the world a new face of robotics—with Asimo as its friendly ambassador.

## Chronology

| | |
|---|---|
| **1956** | Masato Hirose born February 7 in Tochigi Prefecture, Japan |
| **1970s** | Honda begins push for advanced control technology |
| **1980** | Hirose graduates from Utsunomiya University with a degree in precision engineering |
| **1986** | Honda sets up Wako Research center for robotics<br>Hirose goes to work for Honda as a robotics researcher |
| **1987–91** | Honda researchers study dynamic walking in a variety of animals |
| **1994** | P1 appears. It is claimed to be the first true humanoid walking robot |
| **1996** | Hirose's group demonstrates P2, the first fully independent humanoid robot with all computing done on board |
| **1997** | Honda shows the smaller, more agile P3 robot |
| **2000** | Honda reveals Asimo in November |

| 2001 | Hirose becomes senior chief engineer at Honda |
| | Asimo is improved with faster operation and onboard voice recognition software |
| 2002 | An Asimo robot rings the bell at the New York Stock Exchange on February 14 |
| 2004 | Honda reveals a next-generation Asimo whose innovative posture control lets it jog and run |
| 2006 | Asimo robots begin to serve as receptionists and guides |

# Further Reading

## Books

Foerst, Anne. *God in the Machine: What Robots Teach Us about Humanity and God*. New York: Dutton, 2004.
  Discusses the relationship between the quest for artificial intelligence and life and that of various spiritual traditions.
Ichbiah, Daniel. *Robots: From Science Fiction to Technological Revolution*. New York: Harry N. Abrams, 2005.
  Includes a chapter on humanoid and entertainment robots, including Asimo and QRIO.

## Articles

Hara, Yoshiko. "New Industry Awaits Human-Friendly Bipeds: 'Personal Robots' Get Ready to Walk on the Human Side." *Electronic Engineering Times,* 15 September 2002, n.p.
  Includes interviews with Honda and Sony researchers about their humanoid robot projects.
"Next, the Helper." *Asiaweek,* 8 February 2001, n.p.
  Interview with Masato Hirose of Honda Corporation about Asimo and future robots.
Yamaguchi, Yuzo. "All Too Human: Honda's Walking, Talking Robot, Asimo, Leads Automaker into Uncharted Territory." *Automotive News* 76 (January 28, 2002): 100.
  Describes how Asimo has fit into Honda's corporate strategy since the 1970s; also describes how the company sought advice from the Vatican.

## Web Sites

**ASIMO: The Honda Humanoid Robot.** URL: http://world.honda.com/ASIMO. Accessed on July 5, 2005.

Features news and technical background on Asimo, including the history of walking robot research at Honda and the gradual development of locomotion skills.

**Sony Dream Robot: QRIO.** URL: http://www.sony.net/SonyInfo/QRIO. Accessed on September 15, 2005.

Web site for Sony's project to build the ultimate humanoid robot.

# SOCIABLE ROBOTS

## CYNTHIA BREAZEAL AND KISMET

The baby watches the dangling toy with apparent interest—eyes wide, a happy burbling vocalization seeming to convey approval. But when the toy is spun too fast, she scrunches her eyes shut and issues a squeal or two of protest. What brought this change of mood? The new but attentive parent is not sure, but she goes back to dangling the toy slowly. The parent is learning how to play with a baby. The baby is learning how to communicate with other people and negotiate her needs. She is learning how to be a sociable member of the primate species called *Homo sapiens*.

But what if the baby were not a baby, but a robot? This is not a robot that builds something in a factory or a robot that learns how to navigate laboratory corridors. This robot, named Kismet, is helping robotics researcher Cynthia Breazeal learn more about how babies become social creatures—and perhaps how humans and advanced robots can learn from each other.

## In Love with the Droids

Born in Albuquerque, New Mexico, in 1968, Cynthia Breazeal (pronounced like "Brazil") grew up in a high-tech environment when the family moved to California. Her father was a mathematician, and her mother was a computer scientist at the Lawrence Livermore Laboratory. When she was only eight, Breazeal saw the movie *Star Wars* and, as she told Adam Cohen of *Time,* "I just fell in love with the droids. But I was old enough to realize that these kinds of robots didn't exist." Perhaps someday she could build them.

Besides robots, the young Breazeal was also fascinated by medicine and astronomy. When she attended the University of California at Santa Barbara (UCSB), Breazeal considered a future career in the National Aeronautics Space Administration, even the possibility of becoming an astronaut. (The first U.S. woman astronaut, Sally Ride, was frequently in the news at the time.) Breazeal noticed, though, that UCSB also had a robotics center, and there she learned about the work on building planetary robot rovers.

After getting her undergraduate degree in electrical and computer engineering, Breazeal applied for graduate school at the Massachusetts Institute of Technology. She

*MIT researcher Cynthia Breazeal contemplates the robot Kismet in a mirror. This is appropriate, since Kismet is intended to mirror the social interaction by which infants learn.* (©2005 Peter Menzel/menzelphoto.com)

had learned that the MIT robotics lab headed by Rodney Brooks was developing a new generation of small, agile robotic rovers based in part on how insects moved. Breazeal's work on two such robots, named Attila and Hannibal, helped proved the feasibility of mobile robots for planetary exploration, while furnishing a topic for her master's thesis. (This type of robot would be developed further by the Jet Propulsion Laboratory in Pasadena, leading to the *Sojourner* rover that explored Mars in 1997 and the *Spirit* and *Opportunity* rovers that are still going strong on the Martian surface as of 2006.)

Besides its implications for space research, Breazeal's work with Attila and Hannibal demonstrated the feasibility of building robots that were controlled by hundreds of small, interacting programs that detected and responded to specified conditions or "states." It gave concrete reality to Brooks and Breazeal's belief that robots, like living organisms, grew by building more complex behaviors on top of simpler ones, rather than depending on a single top-down design.

## From Cog to Kismet

Breazeal found working on insect-like mobile robots interesting, but her attention was really captured when Brooks announced that he was starting a new project: to make a robot that could interact with people in much the same way people encounter one another socially.

As Breazeal told a *New York Times* interviewer, she saw in Brooks's new project the opportunity to "[bring] robots into human environments so that they can help people in ways that had not been possible before." Possibly, people in turn could "accelerate and enrich the learning processes of machines." Perhaps the robot, rather like a human child, could become "socialized" as it learned appropriate behavior.

The result of the efforts of Brooks and his colleagues (including Breazeal, his new graduate assistant) was the creation of a 6 foot 5 inch (1.96 m) tall robot called Cog. The name, suggested by Breazeal, was short for "cognition," but also meaning a gear in a mechanism, Cog attempted to replicate the sense perceptions and reasoning skills of a human infant. Cog had eyes that focused like those of a person, and, like an infant, could pick up on what people nearby were doing and what they were focused on.

Breazeal had done much of the work in designing Cog's stereo vision system. She and another graduate student also programmed many of the interacting feedback routines that allowed Cog to develop its often intriguing behavior. Cog could focus on and track moving objects and sound sources. Eventually, the robot gained the kind of hand-eye coordination that enabled it to throw and catch a ball and even play rhythms on a snare drum.

One day Breazeal picked up an eraser and waved it in front of Cog. The robot tracked the eraser with its eyes, then reached out and touched it. Breazeal waved the eraser again, and again, Cog reached for and touched it. It was as though Cog and Breazeal were taking turns playing with the eraser. Breazeal realized that there was nothing in the robot's programming that told it about taking turns. This behavior was apparently emerging out of the interaction between the increasingly sophisticated robot and its human partner.

For her doctoral research, Breazeal decided to explore further how a human and a robot might be able to interact using social behavior such as turn-taking. To do so, she again looked toward the human infant as a model. She decided to focus on the key ways in which parents and babies communicate: attention, facial expressions, and vocalization. She designed a smaller robot that would be more childlike and named it Kismet, from a Turkish word meaning fate or fortune.

## Seeing, Hearing, "Speaking"

To many people, the phrase "humanoid robot" conjures up a Hollywood or Disney animatronic replication of a person, with realistic facial features. Kismet, though, looked a bit like the alien from the movie *ET*. The robot was essentially a head without arms or legs. With big eyes (including exaggerated eyebrows), pink ears that could twist, and bendable surgical tubing for lips, Kismet's "body language" conveyed a kind of brush-stroked essence of response and emotion. Kismet had a variety of hardware and software features that supported its interaction with humans.

Like Cogs, Kismet's camera "eyes" functioned much like the human eye. The vision system, though, was more sophisticated than that in the earlier robot. Kismet looked for colorful objects, which were considered to be toys for potential play activities. An even higher priority was given to potential playmates, who were recognized by certain facial features (such as eyes) as well as the presence of flesh tones.

Although Kismet was essentially only a head, the head could tilt forward, conveying interest in a person or thing. To draw people to show interest in return, Breazeal covered Kismet's camera lenses with humanlike artificial eyes, complete with false eyelashes. On the other hand, if a person got too close to the robot (which made vision difficult), Kismet would pull back, conveying body language similar to "you are invading my personal space."

Kismet did not actually understand the words spoken to it. It perceived the intonation and rhythms of human speech and identified them as corresponding to emotional states. If a visitor addressed Kismet with tones of friendly praise (as perhaps one might a baby or a dog), the robot moved to a "happy" emotional

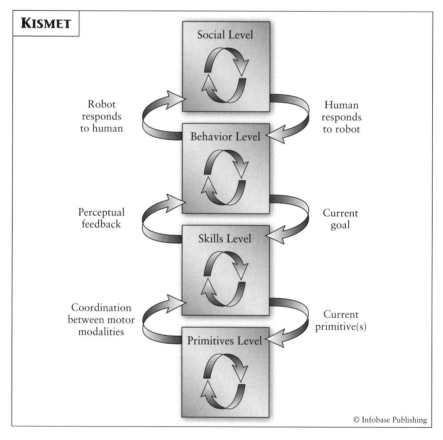

*Kismet had four main levels of behavior. The primitive level tightly coupled sensors and effectors, creating the equivalent of reflexes. The skills level could combine and coordinate motor skills to create more complex movements. The behavior level applied "drives" and other criteria to decide on an overall strategy for behavior. Finally, the social level sought to determine how the robot's human partner would respond.*

## ISSUES: WHAT MIGHT IT MEAN FOR ROBOTS TO "FEEL"?

While skeptics may admit readily to being impressed by the subtle interactions that arose between Kismet and a human visitor, they often raise the question: How can any machine possibly experience emotions in the same way humans, or even the more developed animals, do?

After all, people and other animals are the products of hundreds of millions of years of evolution. Our minds float on a sea of chemistry; animals are fundamentally analog, not digital. Machines, on the other hand, have behavior that is determined by explicit design, however intricate. Any analog behavior must be simulated digitally.

The skeptics' objections can be addressed with another question: How does any person know that other people experience emotions in the same way he or she does? Humans do not have a shared nervous system or (as far as we know) the ability to experience directly the thoughts of others. An individual can only know about another person's state of mind by what is picked up through language, verbal or nonverbal.

There are at least two reasons why people normally grant other people the status of thinking, feeling beings like themselves. Intellectually, it stands to reason that if a being belongs to the same biological species and behaves in similar ways, he or she must have similar emotional states. The most compelling reason to accept that other human beings have real feelings is that we were nurtured by parents who responded to our feelings as though they understood them, while we learned how our feelings were bound up with those of caregivers, teachers, friends, and rivals.

As for robots, even when encountering the relatively simple Kismet, people soon forgot they were dealing with a machine that could be fully described by a series of state and circuit diagrams. As Kismet's descendants become so complex and subtle that no one human can comprehend all of their dynamics, and as our interactions with such robots become increasingly satisfying and useful, we may acknowledge that the robot with whom we are living *feels*—perhaps not exactly as we do, but has feelings that we acknowledge because we *want* to.

ISSUES: WHAT MIGHT IT MEAN FOR ROBOTS TO "FEEL"?
(continued)

At some point then, a robot that combines cognition and "emotional intelligence" to a vastly greater degree than Kismet may receive an implicit acknowledgement of true feeling at least to the degree humans acknowledge the feelings of their canine or feline companions. At this point, any sense of the robot being a fully determined machine will retreat into the realm of abstract theory, just as few people truly believe that humans are completely determined by their genetic expression.

A little later, perhaps, certain robots may be accorded a more or less equivalent status to humanity, perhaps even seen as an intelligent species with whom humans live in symbiosis. And somewhere along this road, if robots become a sort of person, the question of what sort of rights they have will be inevitable.

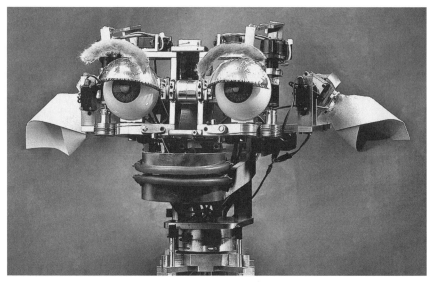

*Looking into Kismet's face, it is hard not to become engaged with the sociable robot.* (©2005 Peter Menzel/menzelphoto.com)

state by smiling. On the other hand, a harsh, scolding tone moved Kismet toward an "unhappy" condition, eliciting a frown. In order to convey the language of facial expressions, Kismet's red rubber "lips" could be controlled by a number of motors. The movements of the eyebrows and ears could also be orchestrated into a variety of expressions connoting such emotional states as

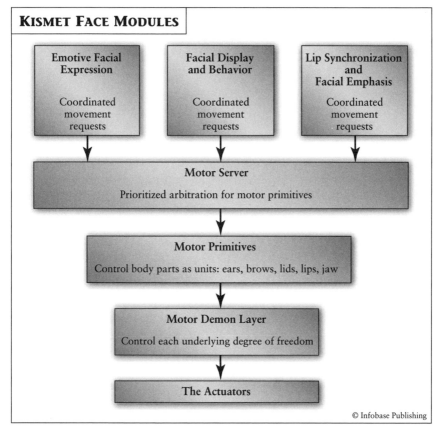

*Kismet's facial expressions were also generated through a layered group of modules. Each of the "expression" routines sent movement commands to the motor server, which determined the order of movements. The requests then went to motor primitives that controlled the individual body parts. Finally, the precise movement commands were given to the individual actuators.*

curiosity, excitement, or boredom. Getting the separate motor controls to work together smoothly proved to be a daunting programming and engineering task.

## Emotional States

Kismet's "emotions" were not just simple indicators of what state the software decided the robot should be in, based on cues it picked up from humans. The robot was so carefully "tuned" in its feedback systems that it established a remarkably natural rhythm of vocalization and visual interaction. Kismet reacted to the human, which in turn elicited further human responses.

---

### PARALLELS: A ROBOTIC GARDEN

Breazeal has created "responsive" robots in new forms and for venues beyond the laboratory. In 2003, the Cooper-Hewitt National Design Museum in New York hosted a "cyberfloral installation" designed by Breazeal. It featured "flowers" of metal and silicone that exhibit behaviors such as swaying and glowing in bright colors when a person's hand comes near. As Breazeal told *New York Times* interviewer Claudia Dreifus:

> The installation communicates my future vision of robot design that is intellectually intriguing and remains true to its technological heritage, but is able to touch us emotionally in the quality of interaction and their responsiveness to us—more like a dance, rather than pushing buttons.

Such robots can intrigue people of all ages and from all backgrounds. Installations such as the robotic garden suggest new possibilities for a fusion of art and technology, as can also be found at the annual Burning Man Festival in the Nevada desert, where artists and technologists collaborate to create elaborate interactive sculptures and join in a communal celebration of creativity.

When Kismet did not have human contact for some time, it became lonely. If a visitor arrived, the robot began an attention-getting display. It tilted its head forward. Its ears swiveled a bit like those of an excited terrier, while its vocal babbling conveyed excitement.

The need for human company was one of Kismet's three major motivational drives. Another was stimulation from seeing "interesting" objects. Because Kismet had no arms, it conveyed its interest in an object to a person, who usually reacted by bringing the object closer to the robot. Like an infant, Kismet also got "tired" after prolonged interaction because of its fatigue drive.

In an interview with Douglas Whynott and Fenella Saunders of *Discover* magazine, Breazeal stressed that

> *The behavior [of Kismet] is not canned. It is being computed and is not a random thing. The interaction is rich enough so that you can't tell what's going to happen next. The overarching behavior is that the robot is seeking someone out, but the internal factors are changing all the time.*

Perhaps the most remarkable thing was how fluidly Kismet's behavior arose out of a system that has 15 separate computers running several different operating systems.

## Leonardo

Seeing how much can be elicited in both robots and humans even by the relatively simple Kismet, Breazeal was eager to build on that experience. One important challenge she faced was to link the cognitive and learning processes to the emotional drives and social interactions. Thus, as she explained to *Time* reporter Adam Cohen in 2000, a future "sociable robot" would learn language much in the way an infant does. The words it would learn most quickly would therefore be those that are connected with emotional needs—being able to ask for a favorite toy, for example. In the article, Breazeal said she hopes that eventually a robot will be able to make the kinds of links that seem to be almost instinctive in toddlers: "When I'm in this state, I can take this action that leads to the person's taking this behavior and getting my needs satiated."

Breazeal's latest robot creation is called Leonardo. Unlike Kismet, Leonardo has a full torso with arms and legs and looks like a furry little *Star Wars* alien. With the aid of artificial skin and an array of 32 separate motors, Leonardo's facial expressions are much more humanlike than Kismet's. Its body language now includes shrugs.

Leonardo's learning capabilities are new and impressive. The robot can learn new concepts and tasks both by interacting with a human teacher and by imitating what it sees people do, starting with facial expressions and simple games.

In the movie *A.I.: Artificial Intelligence* (2001), director Steven Spielberg retold the fairy tale of Pinocchio through an artificially intelligent robot that looks like a little boy. This is a robot that can love—indeed, that needs to love. Although only partially successful, the film gave an idea of the promising but troubling relationships between emotional robots and humans in the not too distant future. The beginnings of that future can be seen in the laboratory today as people respond to Kismet, Leonardo, and their successors.

## The Future of Sociable Robots

In 2002, Breazeal published *Designing Sociable Robots* as a guide to the many dynamic processes that interact in Kismet to produce its complex behavior. She also draws some important conclusions that can guide the future of this exciting new aspect of robotics. For example, her observations of interactions between Kismet and a variety of students and colleagues suggest that robots may advance much more quickly toward fully humanoid status if they can draw humans into interacting with them.

In recent years, a number of developments in robotics has brought closer the day when robots can help with many aspects of daily life. These advances include walking with agility, the ability to navigate sure-footedly in a chaotic world, and a better ability to recognize and manipulate objects in the environment.

Thanks to the work begun by Cynthia Breazeal, researchers can add a new component: the ability to recognize and respond to human emotional language.

Recent writers have suggested that "emotional intelligence"—the ability to assess accurately and respond to one's own emotions and those of others—may be as important as IQ. If advanced emotional intelligence combines with more traditional capabilities, a sociable robot may be able to help people in ways that are barely conceivable today, including the following:

## SOCIAL IMPACT: WOMEN IN ROBOTICS

Robotics has traditionally been considered a form of engineering, a field with relatively low participation by women. When asked why there are so few women in robotics, Breazeal told Adam Cohen of *Time* that women do not get enough support: "Girls aren't discouraged, but they aren't encouraged either." Breazeal also pointed to the lack of women engineers to serve as potential role models for girls. (She noted, however, that in her case her mathematician mother did serve as such a model.) In recent years, Breazeal has begun to intrigue and inspire young women who might be considering careers in robotics.

A more subtle and perhaps more significant impact of Breazeal's work on women in science is how it offers a different vision of what engineers and physical scientists do. Most people see little relationship between engineering and such fields as child psychology or sociology. Even robotics and artificial intelligence, while bringing biology, neurology, and cognitive science into the mix, have not really addressed how robots might relate to peoples' social needs and expectations. By designing robots that engage in social interaction and that learn from their encounters with people, Breazeal is giving technology a new face. This in turn may build a bridge between robotics and such fields as psychology and social science, which have generally appealed more to women. Finally, technologists of both genders may be challenged to think about technology not only in terms of how it might be used but also by how both people and increasingly sophisticated machines may be changing each other.

- A babysitting robot could provide a toddler with a variety of enriching interactions while knowing when the baby is getting tired and should rest
- Robotic teachers might help older children with hand-eye coordination and other manipulation skills, mixing in different activities if the child shows signs of boredom
- Robotic caregivers for older people would be able to not only fetch items and give reminders about medication but also recognize signs of depression or other distress
- Alzheimer's patients could receive memory reinforcement and cognitive enrichment activities, as well as orientation and emotional reassurance
- Specially adapted sociable robots might help stroke victims regain speech and motor skills
- Robots could provide persons suffering from severe cognitive disorders such as autism with carefully monitored and graduated activities to make them better oriented to their environment and more responsive to other people

## "A Robot That Can Be Your Friend"

Besides earning her a doctoral degree from MIT in 2000, Breazeal's work has brought her considerable acclaim. She has been widely recognized as being a significant young inventor or innovator, such as by *Time* magazine and the *Boston Business Forward*. Breazeal was one of 100 "young innovators" featured in MIT's *Technology Review*. She also served as a special consultant for the Steven Spielberg/Stanley Kubrick movie, *A.I.: Artificial Intelligence*.

Today Breazeal is an assistant professor of media arts and sciences at the MIT Media Lab, as well as being director of the lab's Robotic Life Group. Whatever directions her work may take her in the future, Cynthia Breazeal has helped people to see robots not only as tools but also as potential partners. Or, as Breazeal puts it in the *Discover* interview: "The ultimate milestone is a robot that can be your friend."

Breazeal likely misses one friend, though. Kismet first showed her that a robot could become more than a tool or a helper—a true companion. Kismet has since been "retired" and is in an exhibit at the MIT museum.

## Chronology

| | |
|---|---|
| **1968** | Cynthia Breazeal born in Albuquerque, New Mexico, but her family soon moves to Livermore, California |
| **1976** | Breazeal sees *Star Wars* and is intrigued by R2D2 and C3PO |
| **1989** | Breazeal earns a B.S. in electrical and computer engineering from the University of California at Santa Barbara |
| **1992** | Breazeal develops program routines for the walking robots Attila and Hannibal |
| **1993** | Breazeal receives a master's degree in electrical engineering and computer science from the Massachusetts Institute of Technology |
| **1997** | Breazeal begins to design Kismet, the first "sociable robot" |
| **2000** | Breazeal describes the operation of Kismet for her Ph.D. thesis and receives her doctorate in electrical engineering and computer science from MIT |
| **2002** | Breazeal publishes *Designing Sociable Robots* |
| **2003** | Breazeal installs a "cyberfloral installation" of interactive flowers that respond to human presence in a New York art museum |
| **2006** | Breazeal heads the Robotic Life Group at the MIT Media Lab and continues development of the robot "Leonardo" |

# Further Reading

## Books

Breazeal, Cynthia. *Designing Sociable Robots.* Cambridge, Mass.: MIT Press, 2002.

Focusing primarily on the famous robot Kismet, this accessible book explains the many design issues and parameters involved in building robots that can interact in humanlike ways, including sensory, motivational, emotional, behavioral, and facial expression systems.

Brooks, Rodney. *Flesh and Machines: How Robots Will Change Us.* New York: Pantheon Books, 2002.

Cynthia Breazeal's mentor, Rodney Brooks, describes his research and how he came to develop the idea of "situated" and "embodied" robots with a layered architecture of behaviors.

## Articles

Cohen, Adam. "The Machine Nurturer." *Time,* 4 December 2000, pp. 110 ff.

Includes an interview with Cynthia Breazeal and good background on Kismet.

Dreifus, Claudia. "A Passion to Build a Better Robot, One with Social Skills and a Smile." *New York Times,* 10 June 2003, p. F3.

Another interview with Cynthia Breazeal.

Whynott, Douglas, and Fenella Saunders. "The Robot That Loves People." *Discover,* October 1999, p. 66.

Describes encounters with the robot Kismet.

## Web Sites

**Cynthia Breazeal.** URL: http://web.media.mit.edu/~cynthiab. Accessed on September 3, 2005.

Home page at the MIT Media Lab Robotic Life Group; includes summaries of research and downloadable movies of Kismet in action.

**Robotic Life.** URL: http://robotic.media.mit.edu. Accessed on September 3, 2005.

Home page for the Robotic Life Group at the MIT Media Lab; includes introduction to its mission and ongoing research projects, including the robot Leonardo (under "Sociable Robots").

# RADICAL ROBOTICIST

## HANS MORAVEC AND THE FUTURE OF ROBOTICS

Personal computer users can relate: Every couple years or so, it seems that new technologies necessitate a computer ugrade—Windows or Mac, desktop or laptop. Each new PC costs a bit less than the supposedly obsolete model and always seems to have about twice the processor speed and storage capacity.

Carnegie Mellon University robotics researcher Hans Moravec has stated in numerous writings, starting with his book *Mind Children* (1988), that the same thing is now happening to robots. Although the processing needed for robots to function in the real world is vastly more intensive than that found in most computer software, Moravec believes that robots are catching up with the exponential growth that has been characteristic of PCs. This may mean that the high school students of today may be served in

*Hans Moravec has made important contributions to many aspects of robotics, including vision and navigation. Today, though, he is perhaps best known for his speculations on the future development of robotics and the fate of humans in a world of intelligent machines.* (Photo courtesy of Hans Moravec)

**131**

their retirement years by robotic assistants with nearly human-level intelligence. Beyond that, Moravec suggests that the most advanced robots may exceed human intelligence on the same scale that human intelligence surpasses that of chimpanzees.

## At Home with Robots

Hans Moravec was born in the town of Kautzen, Austria, on November 30, 1948. His father was an electronics technician. In 1953, the family moved to Montreal, Canada, where Moravec spent most of his childhood.

Moravec built his first robot when he was only 10 years old. It was built mainly of tin cans, but it was equipped with lights and an electric motor. In high school, Moravec won prizes for his science fair entries—including a mobile robot that could follow light sources and a programmable robot manipulator arm.

In his undergraduate work, Moravec focused on systems for programming and controlling robots. At the time, computers were still too large to put inside a robot, and robots had to be controlled by computer links. Moravec received his bachelor's degree in mathematics from Acadia University in Nova Scotia in 1969.

For his master's degree (awarded in 1971 by the University of Western Ontario), Moravec built a minicomputer-controlled robot that had light and other sensors for responding to the environment. Moravec's master's thesis proposed an extension of LISP (List Processor), the most widely used artificial intelligence programming language, which would be better suited for programming robots.

## Robots à la Carte

In 1971, Moravec moved from Canada to the United States, where he would spend the decade at Stanford University, one of the top centers of American robotics research. By 1973, Moravec was heavily involved with the further development of the Stanford Cart, a remote controlled, wheeled mobile robot that resembled a small table with bicycle wheels. The robot sent images from a television camera back to its controlling computer. Mobile robotics had become an exciting and promising field, as shown by the funding of Cart research by the Defense Advanced Research Projects Agency (DARPA), the National Science Foundation, and the National Aeronautics and Space Administration.

*The Stanford Cart, photographed some time during the 1970s. The rather humble-looking robot was the test bed for pioneering work in mobile robot navigation.* (Photo courtesy of Rodney Brooks)

The Cart's control program had several subroutines. One, called the interest operator, tried to identify "regions of interest" in one of a series of photographs taken by the Cart's camera. (For example, these might be places where there were edges indicating objects and thus potential obstacles.) The correlator routine then looked for matching features in another picture. The camera-solver routine then triangulated the shifted positions between the two pictures in order to determine the distance to the objects of interest. (This is a process that human eyes can perform in a fraction of a second.)

Once the obstacles had been identified and located, the navigator routine planned a path to the destination that avoided the obstacles. The path was then translated into driving instructions that moved the Cart about three feet (1 m) along the path. Another set of pictures was then taken, and the process would be repeated until the Cart reached its destination. The relative slowness of the available minicomputers at the time meant that the Cart drove in a jerky fashion, with 10 to 15 minutes between movements.

The Cart was the first autonomous mobile robot that could plot paths around obstacles, but if one could see the world as the robot saw it, there would be no objects as such, or even wireframe outlines.

Rather, there were clusters, or "clouds," of features that corresponded in a rough way to the actual boundaries of the obstacles. While the Cart usually negotiated cluttered rooms successfully, it sometimes misread the orientation of an object or got stuck in repeated attempts to fit itself through a narrow space. The camera system could also fail to identify objects whose edges lacked sufficient contrast.

When taken outdoors, the Cart faced additional challenges. Moravec and his fellow researchers discovered that because the robot moved so slowly, the shadows of objects would move up to a foot and a half (half a meter) between snapshots. The shadows, which often had a higher contrast than the edges of objects themselves, would then be mistaken for object boundaries.

## I WAS THERE: MORAVEC THE HACKER

Projects such as the Stanford Cart (as well as anything involving images or graphics) required large amounts of computer time. Unfortunately, the limited amount of computer power (much less than on a single desktop machine today) had to be shared by many researchers. Like their counterparts at MIT, the Stanford computer users would keep strange hours to take advantage of "slack time" on the machines. The term *hacker* came to be applied to such users who developed sophisticated tricks to wring the last byte of useful work out of the machines.

Moravec went further than even most hackers. By the late 1970s, he was spending so much time at the computer in the Stanford Artificial Intelligence Lab (SAIL) that he slept by day in a little cubbyhole that he had constructed in the building's rafters, emerging late at night when the computer system was idle.

When he was online, Moravec arranged to have friends bring him groceries so he did not have to leave the keyboard to eat. Moravec's eccentric behavior was less impressive, though, than the storm of ideas with which he pelted his colleagues. According to Rodney Brooks, these included space elevators, huge parallel-processing computers, and even the transfer of human consciousness into machines.

# Robotic Vehicles

Moravec moved to Carnegie Mellon University (CMU) in Pittsburgh in 1980 as a research scientist. He was promoted to senior research scientist in 1985 and principal research scientist in 1993. For his first project at CMU, Moravec began to develop a successor to the Stanford Cart: the CMU Rover. Unlike the Stanford Cart, the Rover carried a dozen or so computer processors on board, although the heavy-duty image processing was still handled by a minicomputer on a remote link. In addition to a TV camera, the Rover included infrared and sonar sensors. The robot was about three feet (1 m) tall and weighed 198 pounds (90 kg). New image-processing arrays made picture analysis about a hundred times faster than with the old Cart.

In 1984, Moravec and his team began a contract to develop a sonar navigation system for Denning Mobile Robotics. Since the sonar provided distance information but could not localize an object within its 30-degree-wide beam, Moravec and graduate student Alberto Elfes devised a different approach to avoiding obstacles. A three-dimensional grid around the robot was used to plot the possibility that an object may exist in a given cell. The result of successive "pings" generated a sort of probability map, which was later extended to combine sonar and visual data. Finally, an algorithm was developed by which the robot could improve its picture of the world by comparing it to a simulated map. Essentially, the result of all this processing was that the robot did not try to avoid obstacles, rather to determine a route that was safely free of them. By the early 1990s, the availability of new supercomputers such as the CM-5 "Connection Machine" improved the accuracy of this grid-based navigation system steadily, and progress continued through the decade.

Moravec's Carnegie Mellon lab also worked on a series of self-driving vehicles. The earliest version, the 1984 Terragator, could roll along jogging trails at about three feet (1 m) per second. Sometimes, however, the remote-control computer would confuse a tree trunk with the road and the Terragator would try to climb it!

Navlab, the first of a new series, begun in 1986, was a big blue truck full of bulky computer gear. It used algorithms to try to pick out the boundaries between the road and surrounding terrain. It gradually improved its ability to stay on the road at faster speeds, up to about 20 miles (32 km) per hour.

Navlab 2, built in 1990 and converted from a military Humvee, introduced a new navigation system. A neural net was "trained" to drive by being shown simulated scenes or video footage from human road trips.

In 1995, Navlab 5 drove across the country from Washington, D.C., to San Diego, California, at an average speed of over 62 miles (100 km) per hour. By now all the computing power needed could be provided by an ordinary laptop computer. (The need for computation was also reduced by having an extensive library of road types and vectors representing angles and curves in the road.) The accompanying human driver had to take control less than 2 percent of the time.

A tougher driving challenge for robots has been provided by the annual races sponsored by the Defense Advanced Research Projects Agency (DARPA). The 132-mile course is a twisting path through Mojave desert and mountain passes similar to the terrain that might be encountered by military vehicles in Afghanistan or Iraq.

In the 2004 race, none of the robotic contestants managed to finish the course, but in October 2005, five of the 23 autonomous vehicles reached the finish line. The winner, with a time of six hours and 53 minutes, was "Stanley," a Volkswagen SUV modified by a Stanford University team with an array of lasers, cameras, and other sensors controlled by an onboard computer.

# Moore's Law and the Quest for Robot Intelligence

Moravec is not only a leading robotics researcher but also a writer whose popular books *Mind Children: The Future of Robot and Human Intelligence* (1988) and *Robot: Mere Machine to Transcendent Mind* (1999) offer a provocative look at the possible future of robotics. To understand Moravec's predictions, it is first necessary to look at how computing power has increased over time—and when it may reach the point where robots transcend human capabilities.

## SOLVING PROBLEMS: IN THE DRIVER'S SEAT

The work being done at Carnegie Mellon University and elsewhere on robot driving systems has many potential uses. Eventually, if systems can be made safe enough, self-driving cars could greatly improve the nation's most popular form of transportation—the automobile. Special freeway lanes may be set aside for automatic driving, and the computers could optimize traffic into a smooth flow and maintain fuel-efficient speeds. The human driver could become a passenger, free to catch up with some work or just enjoy the scenery.

In the late 1990s, the National Automated Highway System Research Program, a consortium of government agencies and private corporations, demonstrated the feasibility of automated cars. A number of serious obstacles remain. For example, if the carrying capacity of highways is greatly increased by automation, what happens when all those extra cars exit from the highway to already congested surface streets? In general, the interaction between automatic and manual drivers remains a problem: Tests of recent Navlab vehicles showed that the computer could react to road conditions much faster than human drivers but was not as good at predicting what those crazy human drivers might do!

The most likely practical results of the automatic driving research will be technologies that assist but do not eliminate the human driver. For years to come, increasingly sophisticated "cruise controls" and systems that can warn inattentive human drivers that they are starting to veer out of their lane or are getting too close to other traffic will appear.

Looking back from the perspective of 2003, Moravec, in his paper for the Association of Computing Machinery, "Robots, After All," acknowledges that researchers in the 1970s and 1980s underestimated greatly the visual processing capacity of the human brain. During those two decades, even the seemingly powerful computers in the leading laboratories could only perform about 1 MIPS (million instructions per second). Moravec notes that

*Though spectacular underachievers at the wacky new stunt of long-hand calculation, we are veteran overachievers at perception and navigation. Our ancestors, across hundreds of millions of years, prevailed by being frontrunners in the competition to find food, escape*

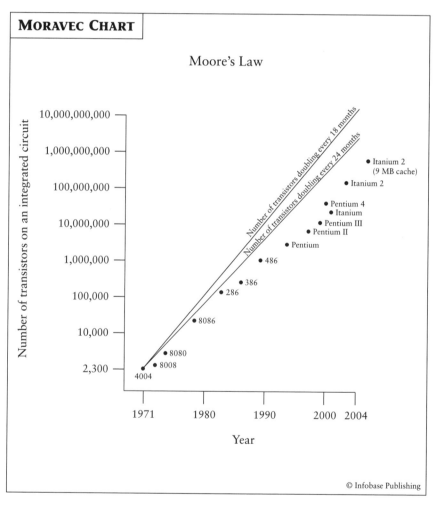

**MORAVEC CHART**

Moore's Law

© Infobase Publishing

*This chart shows how Hans Moravec suggests robotic capabilities have developed since the 1950s, and may develop during the coming decades. The animals in the right column are intended to show rough equivalents in biological brainpower.*

## ISSUES: MORAVEC V. BROOKS

Sheer processing power may not be the decisive factor in achieving humanlike robot intelligence. The way in which processing is organized within the robot may be just as important, as may be the possibility of using a group of cooperating robots instead of a single machine.

Both Rodney Brooks and Hans Moravec have made impressive achievements in developing sophisticated robots that can navigate within and interact with a complex, changing environment. Moravec's approach focuses on visual processing and the ability to create rich three-dimensional models. For example, Moravec sees his cleaning machines as being intelligent and able to analyze each room and plan efficient routes. Gradually, new attachments and capabilities would be added so the cleaning robot could pick up and put away objects (such as children's toys), as well as scrub, mop, or polish as appropriate to the surface and type of dirt.

By comparison, Rodney Brooks's "subsumption architecture," as embodied in the Roomba robotic vacuum cleaner, is based on identifying and implementing those behaviors that, in combination, will accomplish the desired task. A Roomba has no map of its surroundings; it does not calculate optimal paths. It combines long random sweeps and certain special modes (edge-following and spiraling) that when combined do a good job of covering the entire areas while focusing on the spots most in need of cleaning. Where Moravec sees a single, increasingly sophisticated cleaning robot, Brooks (and his colleagues Colin Angle and Helen Greiner) suggests in his book *Flesh and Machines* that "flocks" or entire "ecologies" of simpler, Roomba-like robots could each perform particular chores of mopping, scrubbing, and so on.

While these two approaches to robotics seem very different, they could well be complementary in many ways. Many simpler tasks may be suitable for the Roomba-style robots, while others might require a single, sophisticated robot more like what Moravec envisages. For example, suppose the army needs to secure and make safe an area that is likely to have mines or improvised explosive devices. A flock of simple robots might be able to find and identify the mines and bombs. A sophisticated robot could then go to each device, determine which type of tool or manipulator to use, and disarm it safely. As a practical matter, many robot designs use both top-down, centralized and bottom-up, distributed approaches.

*danger and protect offspring. Existing robot-controlling computers are far too feeble to match this massive ultra-optimized perceptual inheritance.*

The retina of the human eye packs together millions of cells that can detect the edges of objects and react to motion. Making a rough calculation, Moravec concludes that even the 1,000 MIPS (one billion calculations per second) capacity of a late 1990s supercomputer falls far short of the processing occurring in the retina and optic nerve, let alone the human brain itself, which may perform processing equivalent to about 100 million MIPS (or 100 trillion instructions per second)! By comparison, Moravec estimates that a 2003 model desktop computer has a processing power equivalent to the nervous system of an insect or perhaps the brain of a guppy.

Against this formidable processing gap between computer and brain must be placed Moore's Law, the well-attested observation (by pioneer chip-builder Gordon Moore) that the processing power of the top-of-the-line computer chip roughly doubles every 18 months to two years. If this trend continues, Moravec believes that computers (and their associated robots) could reach humanlike processing capacity by 2040. And because this growth is driven by geometrical (doubling) functions, humans might be quickly surpassed after that time.

## Robots: The Next Generations

Today's robots can, at their best, do only a few things well. They are specialists. Moravec suggests that by around 2020 the first true "universal" robots may appear. Just as a computer is a universal machine in that it can perform any kind of calculation for which it has been given the appropriate instructions, a universal robot could be given programs enabling it to tidy or clean a house, wash dishes, mow lawns, take inventory in a warehouse, guard that warehouse, or even play games with children. Moravec sees this first generation of universal robots as having about a 10,000 MIPS processing power and "minds" equivalent in complexity to that of a lizard.

The first generation of universal robots will work in rather constrained environments. They may learn more about their surroundings in terms of navigation, but it will essentially perform their tasks

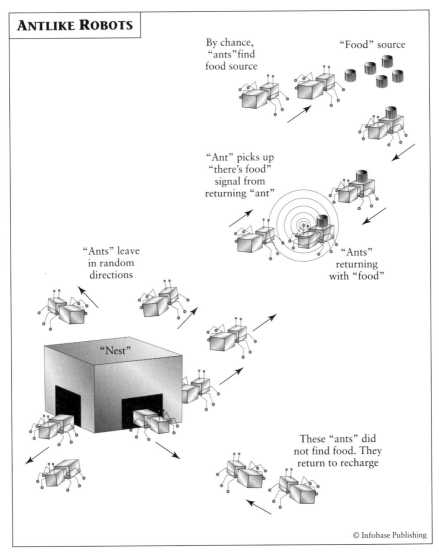

**ANTLIKE ROBOTS**

By chance, "ants" find food source

"Food" source

"Ant" picks up "there's food" signal from returning "ant"

"Ants" leave in random directions

"Ants" returning with "food"

"Nest"

These "ants" did not find food. They return to recharge

© Infobase Publishing

*A swarm of antlike robots may one day be designed to cooperate to accomplish a task. In this schematic, the robots organize a search for "food" objects.*

by rote. Moravec foresees a second generation of universal robots with a processing power of 30,000 MIPS (roughly equivalent to a mouse brain). These second-generation robots would be equipped with learning or "conditioning" modules that would reinforce those approaches to a task that work best. ("Best" might be defined as a combination of efficiency, low energy use, and lack of damage through mishaps.)

Moravec's third generation of robots (10 million MIPS or a monkey equivalent) would have a big boost of cognitive power. They would have a database that includes physics and physical properties of objects, "knowing" how humans use and refer to objects, and some grasp of human psychology and behavior.

The fourth generation would reach humanlike processing levels (300 million MIPS), would be comfortable with abstractions, and could apply its reasoning to any domain in which it finds itself.

## Meanwhile, Back at the Warehouse

By 2003, Moravec had a reputation as a way-out futurist. Together with inventor and artificial intelligence pioneer Ray Kurzweil, Moravec was associated with ideas such as robots that could produce anything desired or perform any service required, not to mention the possibility that humans could download their minds into humanoid robots and achieve virtual immortality. Such talk made for popular lectures and media interest, but Moravec then surprised a number of observers by taking on a more practical challenge.

Robots, after all, do not need to be as smart as people to be *useful* to people. In a *Scientific American* article, Moravec said that he expects that self-navigating mobile robots, for example, will become increasingly prevalent during the next decade. Pursuing this vision, Moravec cofounded SEEGRID Corporation in 2003. (As he told *Scientific American* writer Chip Walter, "It was time. The computing power is here.")

The roots for the new technology were in Moravec's proposal for an advanced mobile robot vision system, which was funded in

## SOCIAL IMPACT: TRANSCENDENCE THROUGH TECHNOLOGY?

The ideas of the more radical robot theorists (including, to some extent, Hans Moravec and even Rodney Brooks) share elements of a new future-oriented philosophy that has been called extropianism or transhumanism. The basic elements of this philosophy include a belief that humans can increasingly master technologies that will lead to expanded mental capabilities, ultimate control over matter and energy, and even immortality. Some followers of extropian philosophy see advanced robotics as the way to create new bodies into which human minds may someday be downloaded or transplanted. Others prefer to focus on genetics and the use of cloning or other techniques. Nanotechnology, or the ability to build materials atom-by-atom, is also seen as a way to get beyond existing limits on energy and natural resources.

Entropy can be thought of as the "running down" of the universe, leading to a gradual loss of useful energy or of information. Established physics states that entropy is the ultimate fate of the universe. Extropy, therefore, suggests an opposite trend: an open-ended, potentially infinite increase in information, capacity, and consciousness. Similarly, those who prefer the term *transhumanism* see it as a going beyond the physical and cognitive limits of the present human species.

Such philosophies are not new—they echo such thinkers as the German philosopher Friedrich Nietzsche and his celebration of the "superman" and the political movement called technocracy that achieved some influence in the early to mid-20th century. The extropians, however, claim that the necessary technology for transcendent humanity is nearly at hand. They argue that artificial intelligence, advanced robots, and genetically enhanced humans will be here soon, like it or not, so people should figure out how to use these technologies intelligently—and indeed, use them to increase human intelligence so we can cope with them.

1998 by the U.S. Defense Advanced Research Projects Agency for $970,000. By 2002, a successful demonstration system had been completed.

The basic idea for the SEEGRID Corporation's first product was a delivery cart that the user "trained" by bringing it to required locations while it recorded three-dimensional images and calculated safe routes from one location to the next. The robot could then travel automatically between the locations and await loading or unloading by humans. Its sophisticated three-dimensional stereo-vision mapping system automatically updated its internal maps and calculated new routes or detours if necessary. In the *Scientific American* article, Moravec said that he sees other applications for such robots, including housecleaning. SEEGRID and E-P Equipment Inc. announced the first implementation of this system in a warehouse delivery vehicle called "Smarttruck" in January 2005.

Such vehicles have a large potential market. Currently, workers must laboriously use dollies or forklifts to move materials into or out of warehouses. Some existing automated systems (such as that used by the giant bookstore Amazon) use fixed conveyer belts or guideways. Such systems are prone to blockage from unexpected movements of materials, and they are not easy to reconfigure as the flow of work changes. Moravec's robotic stevedores can find their way around most obstacles. If the layout of the warehouse or factory changes, the robots are simply "walked" along the new path and told about the new designated delivery points.

## Looking Forward

Today Moravec continues as director of the Mobile Robot Laboratory at Carnegie Mellon University and directs innovative projects in robotic vision and other applications. He has also consulted for a number of leading computer and robotics companies and the Office of Naval Research and lectured widely at universities and conferences.

When Chip Walter of *Scientific American* asked Moravec what he thought would happen when robots became more intelligent than people, he observed that "something like 99 percent of all species go extinct." Would this be the fate of humanity as well? Maybe, but Moravec suggested a different possibility. Calling future robots our "mind children," Moravec speculated that advanced robots might care for humanity out of a sense of affinity or obligation, perhaps as children try to provide for the needs of their aging parents. Perhaps all humans' needs will be provided for, except the need to be useful. It is a sobering thought.

## Chronology

| | |
|---|---|
| **1948** | Hans Moravec born November 30 in Kautzen, Austria |
| **1953** | Moravec's family emigrates to Canada |
| **1958** | Moravec builds his first mobile robot at the age of 10 |
| **1965–67** | Moravec attends Loyola College |
| **1969** | Moravec receives his bachelor's degree from Acadia University in Nova Scotia |
| **1971** | Moravec receives his master's of science degree from the University of Western Ontario |
| | Moravec moves to the United States and attends Stanford University, where he later works with the Stanford Cart |
| **1980** | Moravec is awarded his Ph.D. by Stanford University |
| | Moravec begins his career at Carnegie Mellon University (CMU) and organizes the Mobile Robot Lab |
| **1980s** | Moravec works on CMU Rover, a much-improved successor to the Stanford Cart |
| **1984** | Moravec and students begin working on sonar-based grid navigation systems |
| **1988** | Moravec's book *Mind Children* predicts human-level robots in a generation or so |
| **1990s** | Navlabs demonstrate the ability of robot-controlled vehicles to drive on real roads |
| **1998** | Moravec revisits the future in *Robot: Mere Machine to Transcendent Mind* |

| 2003 | Moravec cofounds SEEGRID Corporation (with Scott Friedman) to develop commercial applications for mobile robots |
|---|---|
| 2005 | SEEGRID announces that the "Smarttruck" robot will be used for work in warehouses |

# Further Reading

## Books

Brooks, Rodney. *Flesh and Machines: How Robots Will Change Us.* New York: Panethon Books, 2002.
> This description of Brooks's robotics theories and experiments nicely complements the accounts of Moravec's work. The two researchers share many ideas but also have differences in approach and attitude.

Moravec, Hans. *Mind Children: The Future of Robot and Human Intelligence.* Cambridge, Mass.: Harvard University Press, 1988.
> Moravec predicts a radical increase in the power of artificial intelligence and its overshadowing of humanity; however, reality during the following decade fell somewhat short of the predictions.

———. *Robot: Mere Machine to Transcendent Mind.* New York: Oxford University Press, 1999.
> Moravec updates and elaborates predictions of robotics advances; suggests robots will match human intelligence by 2040 and surpass it by 2050.

## Articles

Moravec, Hans. "Robots, After All." *Communications of the ACM* 46 (October 2003): 90–97. Available online. URL: http://www.frc. ri.cmu.edu/~hpm/project.archive/robot.papers/2003/CACM.2003. html. Accessed on September 10, 2005.
> Describes the slow but now accelerating progress of robotics in recent decades.

———. "The Stanford Cart and the CMU Rover." Robotics Institute, Carnegie Mellon University. February 1983. Available online. URL: http://cart.frc.ri.cmu.edu/users/hpm/project.archive/robot. papers/1983/ieee83.mss. Accessed on September 12, 2005.
> Moravec describes his extensive involvement with developing two mobile robots in the 1970s and early 1980s.

"Stanford Team Wins Robot Race." MSNBC.com. Available online.
  URL: http://www.msnbc.msn.com/id/9621761. Accessed on
  October 19, 2005.
    Describes the 2005 DARPA "Grand Challenge" in the Mojave des-
    ert.
Walter, Chip. "You, Robot." *Scientific American* 292 (January
  2005): 36–37A.
    Describes SEEGRID, Moravec's new robotics firm, and also Moravec's
    predictions about future generations of robots.

## Web Sites

**Extropy Institute.** URL: http://www.extropy.org. Accessed on October
  12, 2005.
    An organization dedicated to transcending human limitations (and
    even mortality) through technology, including robotics.
**Hans Moravec.** URL: http://www.frc.ri.cmu.edu/~hpm. Accessed on
  October 10, 2005.
    Home page at Carnegie Mellon University; includes an archive of
    Moravec's past robot projects and speculation about the future of
    robots.

# 10

# CYBORG ODYSSEY

## KEVIN WARWICK EXTENDS THE HUMAN BODY

*"We can rebuild him. We have the technology. We have the capability to make the world's first Bionic man. Steve Austin will be that man. Better than he was before. Better . . . stronger . . . faster."*

In the 1970s TV series *The Six Million Dollar Man*, a test pilot who had been badly crippled in a crash is rebuilt with bionic limbs and implants, enabling him to become an intelligence agent with unique capabilities. Three decades later, there are still no people who can run 60 miles an hour or lift cars with their bare hands. The first steps toward extending the human nervous system and linking it to robots have already been taken, however, and they have much more interesting implications than just speed or brute strength. In 2002, Kevin Warwick, a British cybernetics researcher, became the first human to use a neural implant to directly control a robot and to exchange nerve signals with another person.

## Science, Soccer, and Motorcycles

Kevin Warwick was born on February 9, 1954, in Coventry, England. Although his father was a teacher, his grandfather had been a Welsh miner, and the family was only gradually working its way into the middle-class world of detached homes.

As a young boy, Warwick was curious, energetic, and particularly fond of soccer. (He would become a talented amateur player). When

*British robotics researcher Kevin Warwick holds up his cyborg arm. While the implant itself is not visible, Warwick had a friend design a cyberpunkish-looking gauntlet to contain the interface circuitry.* (Photo ©iCube Solutions Inc.)

Warwick was eight, however, his father developed severe agoraphobia, or fear of open spaces. When rest and therapy did not seem to help, the doctors resorted to a neurological operation. (During this period, brain surgery for psychological problems was more prevalent than it is today.)

The surgeons opened small holes in Warwick's father's head and severed some nerve connections. The operation succeeded in removing the agoraphobia. In his autobiography, *I, Cyborg,* Warwick recalled that "It was father's illness and subsequent cure that first prompted me to think objectively about how the human brain operates and what exactly our mental processes are all about." Warwick's fascination with neurology would eventually bear fruit in innovative research.

In grammar school, Warwick became fascinated by science and technology. He enjoyed watching science programs on television and reading about how famous scientists such as Michael Faraday and Humphrey Davies had made their discoveries. By his early teenage years, that interest had expanded to science fiction, including the British television movie *Doctor Who and the Daleks,* where Earth is invaded by malevolent robots who look something like Art Deco salt shakers. Warwick did not fit the nerd stereotype, though—he was fond of activities more in keeping with working-class boys, such as rooting for the Coventry soccer team and earning enough money to buy his own motorcycle.

## Working World and University

After graduating from high school, Warwick also followed more of a working-class path: Instead of going to university, he got a job as an apprentice telephone technician at British Telecom. The work proved to be a pleasing mixture of intellectual challenge and physical labor, such as digging holes and climbing poles. In his spare time, Warwick continued his varied reading. A science fiction novel called *The Terminal Man* by Michael Crichton particularly intrigued Warwick. In the novel, surgeons attempt to change a criminal's behavior through electronically controlled nerve implants. Of course, things go horribly wrong, but Warwick wondered if such technology could be safely developed and used.

Eventually, Warwick felt his telephone job had become a dead end. He obtained the necessary technical certificates, took entrance exams and some technical courses, and in 1976, he enrolled in Aston University in Birmingham, England. He found the three years there to be rewarding, although he had also married, and he and his wife, Sylvia, had to make considerable financial sacrifices. Warwick received his undergraduate degree in 1979 and continued on in the Ph.D. program at Imperial College, London. For his doctoral thesis, he studied ways to monitor and correct industrial production systems automatically.

After a few years as a lecturer at the University of Newcastle and as an Oxford Fellow, Warwick decided to look for a permanent position. When he discovered that a professorship in cybernetics was available at the University of Reading, England, Warwick was excited. By the 1980s, cybernetics, the science of communication and control pioneered by Norbert Wiener, was not commonly pursued as a single unified subject. Rather, research in computer systems and robotics was likely to be parceled out among computer science and various disciplines of electronic and mechanical engineering. But for Warwick, cybernetics evoked the very connections he was most interested in: systems, control, communication, computation, and even biology. In 1988, therefore, Warwick applied for and received the professorship in cybernetics at Reading that he holds today.

## Boosting Productivity

As professor of cybernetics at the University of Reading, Warwick has directed or been involved with a variety of bread-and-butter robotics projects. Some of them drew upon Warwick's past work in developing software that can detect and diagnose faults in automated manufacturing systems. Clearly, such systems are of great practical interest to manufacturers, since maximum throughput with minimum breakdowns results in the highest possible productivity.

One of Warwick's approaches was to use a neural network that can gradually recognize what combinations of factors or data values make a breakdown more likely. Or approaching the problem a different way, the network can look for (and reinforce) those conditions that result in efficient, uninterrupted production. Consulting with some manufacturing companies, Warwick's software was even able to help them pinpoint differences between shifts of human workers in terms of how well they supervised the automatic machinery.

## Helping the Disabled

Warwick's long-term interest in the mechanisms of the human body and their possible enhancement has naturally extended to the possibility of creating devices to help disabled people. He and other researchers at Reading developed, for example, a platform onto which an ordinary wheelchair can be placed. The platform can then be driven with a joystick. It is equipped with ultrasonic sensors and can give warnings such as "Object to the left!"

One day the cybernetics researchers had brought the wheelchair platform to the Avenue School in Reading, a school for children with special needs. Warwick and the researchers who built the platform found it rather awkward to drive since it was not like the automobiles most people are used to. The researchers were worried that the disabled children would have even more trouble with the device.

They were surprised when the first disabled child who tried it out, a boy with cerebral palsy, began zipping the chair around the room at breakneck speed, avoiding all obstacles confidently. The incident suggested to Warwick that disabled people may be better able to adapt to new technology than people who have never had to rely on assistive devices.

In the late 1990s, Warwick and his research team worked on everything from adapting networking and mapping technology to making it easier for disabled persons to function independently at home. In the "Intelligent Home System," doors, windows, and devices such as lights, heaters, and television sets each had a control processor linked to a central processor. The resident could then give vocal or other commands to control all the features of the home.

Mobile robot technology could also enhance mobility for disabled persons. A robot wheelchair could include an internal map with significant locations plus the usual collision-avoidance and path-finding software. The wheelchair user could simply say "take me to the bathroom" or "take me to the kitchen table," and the chair would do the rest. A demonstration model of a "magic" robot chair was built and appeared regularly on the British television show *Jim'll Fix It*. (Interestingly, the show's producers requested that the unit's high-quality synthesized speaking voice be replaced by something that sounded more like a robot!)

## The Seven Dwarfs

Warwick and his fellow researchers at the University of Reading have developed robots with a more open-ended purpose of exploring the architecture of robot intelligence. Some, like "Walter," are

## SOLVING PROBLEMS: SAFER BATHS

One of the projects undertaken by Kevin Warwick's team at the University of Reading illustrates how it is possible to come up with a simpler, lower tech solution to a problem that seems very complicated at first.

The problem was how to enable epileptic persons to bathe alone safely. People with epilepsy usually prefer taking care of their daily needs instead of relying on a companion or attendant for assistance. Epileptic seizures are largely unpredictable, and if one occurs while a person is in the bathtub, it is possible he or she might drown. The Reading team sought a way to detect the onset of a seizure so the water could be quickly drained from the tub.

Epileptic seizures vary greatly in their severity and outward signs. In some cases limbs thrash wildly, while in others the only sign may be a flickering of the eyelids. Although there are characteristic brain waves associated with a seizure, wearing a cap full of sensors and electrodes is awkward—not to mention potentially dangerous in a wet environment.

Warwick devised a simpler solution. He took an ordinary pair of eyeglass frames (without lenses) and attached moisture sensors to them. If a person wearing the glasses has a seizure that causes his or her head to slump into the water, the sensor sends a signal to a relay that opens the drain and empties the bath.

insect-like walking robots. These robots generally follow the "subsumption architecture" first developed by Rodney Brooks. That is, they are decentralized, with layers of behavior ranging from simple avoidance of obstacles to exploration and mapping the world. Each of Walter's legs is separately operated and synchronized by a "heartbeat" signal. If a leg is removed or disabled, the other legs compensate, just as with an insect.

As with humans and other organisms, the brain or central processor in a robot with distributed architecture needs only to send a master signal to start walking or undertake another activity. The lower-level "nervous system" takes care of the rest, allowing the brain to engage in higher-level behavior such as planning. "Elma" is a sleeker, more sophisticated successor to Walter that includes tactile sensors to allow the legs to "feel" the terrain and adjust to it. As the project continued, researchers also added learning routines to help Elma master new skills.

Learning through feedback is the featured activity for a swarm of wheeled robots that also inhabits the lab at Reading. (Since there were originally seven of the robots, they were dubbed "The Seven Dwarfs.") Each robot has two powered wheels and one front wheel that is like a caster. The sturdy little robots emphasized rapid activity rather than cautious exploration.

## "Hello, Mr. Chip"

As interesting as the robotics research at the University of Reading was, by the late 1990s, Kevin Warwick had become increasingly preoccupied with a more daring possibility—that of connecting the human body directly to the cybernetic world of increasingly intelligent machines. He would become his own research subject.

In August 1998, Warwick arranged to have a small silicon chip, about one inch (2.5 cm) long and a tenth of that wide implanted in his arm. The procedure, performed under a local anesthetic, took only about 15 minutes.

There was little remarkable about the chip itself—similar chips have been implanted in pets for years, where they serve to identify strays. What was significant was the way computers in Warwick's building at the university had been programmed to recognize and respond to the chip. As Warwick walked, lights came on, doors opened, and computers displayed his home Web page. Warwick also heard the greeting "Hello, Mr. Warwick, you have mail."

Warwick told *PC World* reporter Jana Sanchez-Klein that he was surprised how quickly he got used to being connected in this way:

*I'm feeling more at one with the computer. It's as though part of me is missing when I'm not in the building. In my house, I have to open doors and turn on lights. I don't feel lonely, but I don't feel complete.*

---

**I WAS THERE: ROBOT BUMPER CARS**

---

Early versions of the University of Reading's "Seven Dwarfs" robots could be rather disconcerting and occasionally dangerous. As Warwick recounted in *March of the Machines:*

> In the pre-Seven Dwarf era, however, even more powerful motors were used, coupled with open gear boxes. These first robots would hurtle around the laboratory at breakneck speed, crashing into walls and doors. They were, therefore, designed with metal bumpers at the front and with a sturdy frame.
>
> Another early problem to overcome was that of stopping a robot once we had started it. Catching a rapid transit autonomous robot with an open gear box, in full flight, was quite dangerous, with a serious chance of injury. More often than not we simply had to wait until the robot's battery had run flat and then reclaim it.

Perhaps the Reading experimenters might have learned from the modern sport of Robot Wars (or Battlebots), in which heavily armed and armored remote-controlled robots engage in the arena in gladiatorial combat. Besides remote controls, these robots are equipped with safety interlocks that can disable the machine without a person having to get too close.

---

Warwick's first tentative step into the world of implants only whetted his appetite for a more profound connection. It would be one in which he would not only be "read" by machines but also would communicate with them directly via the signals in his nervous system. He would take the next big step toward becoming a new type of being—a cyborg.

## From Humans to Cyborgs

The word *cyborg* is short for "cybernetic organism." (A more or less equivalent term is *bionic organism*, meaning biological plus electronic.) A cyborg is a human whose nervous, musculoskeletal, or other systems are integrally enhanced or extended through links to electronic devices.

In a sense, every person who wears glasses, uses a hearing aid, or walks with the aid of a cane is a cyborg. All of these devices extend human physical capabilities in some way. To distinguish users of simple aids from true cyborgs, most theorists require that the devices be integral: that is, permanently attached, as well as linked through sophisticated interactions. For example, a cochlear implant

---

### ISSUES: CONVENIENCE V. PRIVACY

The ability to be continually connected to a network of helpful computers and other devices is certainly convenient. It also provides a taste of "cyborg-ness" by making the technology a more seamless extension of the human mind and senses. In order to create this seamless environment, though, the computer has to know who you are—and if it knows, who else might know, and what might they find out?

The use of radio frequency identification (RFID) chips is becoming more common in store merchandise and even in library books. Many privacy advocates are concerned that the technology will give government snoops and corporate marketers too much information about a person's location, habits, and choices. Defenders of RFID say that the fear is overstated and that the data cannot be read from more than a few feet away.

Thus far there seems to be no rush for people to get their own RFID implants, although a few exclusive nightclubs have provided them to patrons who want to bypass a screening process. It is possible that more people would be interested in an implant if it sped them through usually onerous activities, such as checking in at airports or medical offices. Paroled criminals (particularly sex offenders) might also be considered for the technology, as it could be used to enforce restrictions such as entering school property. The desirability and appropriate restrictions for such surveillance are likely to remain contentious issues for many years to come.

that allows some deaf people to hear is integrally connected to the ear. A prosthetic limb that responds directly to muscular movement or even neural signals could also be considered a step toward becoming a cyborg. There have also been crude but promising experiments where light sensors have been directly connected to the optic nerve, enabling blind people to see low-resolution pictures of objects in their environment.

An ultimate cyborg is likely to have many such devices, intended not only to correct disabilities but also to enhance normal human capabilities greatly or add new abilities entirely. A cyborg potentially combines the best features of humans and robots.

Kevin Warwick has given several reasons why he has undertaken rather risky procedures in order to create the first cybernetic links between the human nervous system and machines. For one thing, Warwick shares with robotics pundits such as Hans Moravec and Rodney Brooks the belief that robots will inevitably surpass humans in intelligence, perhaps in the lifetime of today's high school students.

Warwick suggested in his 2000 letter to the British newspaper the *Guardian* that

> *One realistic alternative to the hand of evolution patting humans on the back in an "it's been nice knowing you" way is for humans to themselves link up much more closely with the circuitry being created. We humans can evolve into cyborgs—part human, part machine.*

This attempt to meet the challenge of a machine-dominated future was not the only reason Warwick wanted to pursue his cyborg quest. Being able to link the human nervous system directly to machines could make great inroads into understanding in detail exactly which nerve signals control which movements, as well as the relationship between thoughts and emotions and nervous activity.

Direct nerve links between persons might finally answer some age-old philosophical questions. As Warwick wrote to the *Guardian,* these include: "When you feel pain is it more or less than my pain? When I think of the color red, is it the same as when you think of it?"

Warwick concluded his *Guardian* letter by saying that he was eager to see what a future as a cyborg might hold. A number of daunting obstacles would first have to be addressed.

# Cyborg 2.0: The Neural Implant Project

The radio implant that Warwick called "Cyborg 1.0" involved a simple operation with no real risks except perhaps infection. "Cyborg 2.0," however, would be a much more radical procedure. It involved exposing the central nerve in Warwick's arm and driving into it an array containing 100 individual electrodes, each a few millimeters in diameter.

If it worked, Warwick and other researchers would be able to amplify and monitor up to 20 separate neural signals at a time. Electrical impulses could also be fired into the implant to create nerve signals that might, for example, flex Warwick's thumb.

The proposed procedure had never been done before, and because the implant penetrated the nerve, it could cause damage—possibly permanent damage. Warwick therefore had to go through an elaborate procedure to obtain approval from a hospital ethics board, as well as deal with issues of legal liability. On top of that, the electrode array the researchers wanted to use was still in development. Warwick decided that he could not tell the manufacturer, Bionic Tech, what he wanted the array for, lest the company refuse to sell him one.

Finally, on March 14, 2002, Warwick went to the Radcliffe Infirmary at Oxford. The surgeon, Peter Teddy, made an incision about two inches (5 cm) up from Warwick's left wrist. He then probed for the median nerve, accidentally sending a sensation like a large electric shock racing up Warwick's arm. After finding the nerve, the surgeon made another incision and threaded a plastic tube called a bodger between the two incisions. (This would link the neural implant with the place where the wires would emerge from Warwick's arm to a connector pad that Warwick called the "gauntlet.") After some difficulty, this was completed. The nerve implant array was then fired . . . but it dropped rather than going into the nerve. It turned out the compressed air hoses to the firing device had been connected wrong. Finally, the array was successfully implanted. Warwick's arm was sewed up.

## Cyborg Experiments

Warwick had to wait nearly two weeks until they would know whether the implant was properly connected to the nerve. When the researchers checked each channel for nerve signals, they found to their relief that 20 of the electrodes were picking up Warwick's nerve signals. During the following two weeks, they painstakingly had Warwick perform various finger movements in order to determine which muscles were associated with particular nerve signals. This work was difficult because often one muscle turned out to involve several overlapping signals. Warwick now had at least the capability to become a sort of cyborg. But what could he actually do? Meanwhile, the media had picked up the story, both in Britain and the United States, though reporters were not sure what the story was all about.

The next logical step was to see whether particular nerve signals from Warwick could be interfaced with devices in the external world. Researchers created an interface unit that translated nerve signals to data signals that could be interpreted by computerized devices. Warwick was eventually able to control computer displays with simple finger movements. More significantly, he demonstrated that he could drive and steer an electric wheelchair with tiny movements, a feat that could have very practical implications for severely paralyzed persons.

Another interesting demonstration involved Warwick controlling an articulated robotic hand, built by Peter Kyberd, using only hand movements. When Warwick made a fist, the signals traveled over the Internet to the hand, which also made a fist. This direct neural remote control opened many exciting possibilities. For example, someday a surgeon might be able to perform operations remotely by connecting his or her hand to a robotic hand. Perhaps even more usefully, nerve signals arriving at an amputee's stump could be directly related to a prosthetic robotic arm or leg, which would truly respond and feel like the real thing!

Warwick and his colleagues performed a number of other interesting experiments during the two months or so the implant was in place. Nerve signals were used to control the way a "swarm" of little robots interacted with each other. And after considerable experimentation, they were able to verify that the connection between Warwick's nervous system and the world was two-way. That is, he could receive electronically generated nerve signals that would cause his muscles to react.

## The Human Connection

There was a final experiment Warwick eagerly wanted to perform. Time was running out: The doctors were afraid that if the implant was left in too long it would begin to fuse with the body and be difficult to remove safely. Also, the electrodes were, for unknown reasons, gradually failing, and only a few remained active.

Irena, Warwick's second wife, wanted very much to share in his exploration of the world of cyborgs. Originally, they thought that she, too, could receive a full implant. Husband and wife would then be able to send nerve impulses directly to each other. The bureaucratic hurdles proved too insurmountable, so they had to settle for Irena having two simple needle electrodes inserted into her median nerve.

Finally, Warwick and Irena's nervous systems were connected. As he recounted in *I, Cyborg*:

> *I waited. It seemed to take an age. But then I felt it, a shot of current, a charge, running down the inside of my left index finger. A beautiful, sweet, deliciously sexy charge. I felt like I had never felt before. I jumped with surprise more than anything else and shouted, "Yes!"*

## An Open Future

In 2000, Warwick gave a series of five Royal Institution lectures under the title "Rise of the Robots." (The lecture series had begun in 1825 by electrical pioneer Michael Faraday.) Warwick's work in organizing school robotics activities was also recognized with the Millennium Award, from the British Engineering and Physical Sciences Research Council. He has also received the Future of Health Technology Award from the Massachusetts Institute of Technology.

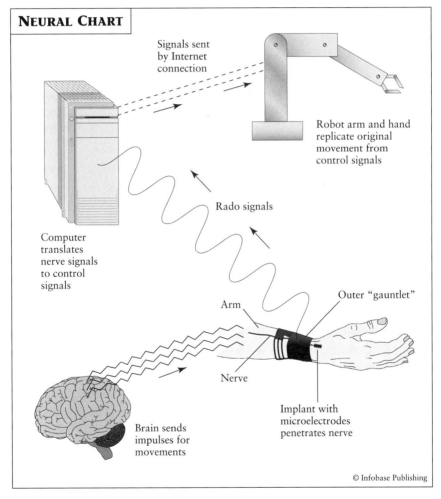

This diagram shows how a neural implant and an Internet connection could be used to control a robot anywhere in the world. No need for a keyboard or mouse!

## Social Impact: "Enhanced" vs. "Normal"

There is little controversy about cyborg technology that gives disabled people fuller capabilities. For example, in a decade or two, implanted electronic devices may be able to route nerve signals around a damaged portion of the spinal cord, enabling a person to walk again. Deaf and visually handicapped people are also likely to be helped considerably by the new digital neural interface technology.

Suppose, though, that after another few decades direct neural implants enable people to tap into computer networks directly. Whether an image is generated via the optic nerve or the information is transferred directly into the brain, the result is that the person has virtually instant access to everything on the World Wide Web—and by then, the Web will probably be millions of times larger than it is today. Such a person could also tap into cameras around the world, extending his or her senses wherever the network can reach. Instant, silent communication would also be available, either through sub-vocalization or through direct transfer of mental images—electronic telepathy.

This is the world of Cyberpunk, a type of science fiction first popularized by William Gibson in his 1984 novel, *Neuromancer.* As he and other writers depicted it, though, human enhancement is at best a mixed blessing. The biggest hitch is that the technology may be expensive and available to relatively few people, just as personal computers in the 1980s were mainly found in middle- and upper-class homes.

In a world where some people are enhanced and others have only their natural mental abilities and senses, class distinctions may widen radically. In recent years, social critics have warned that a digital divide is separating people who have access to the Internet and other technology (and the knowledge of how to use it) and those who do not—disproportionately the poor and minorities. Could enhanced and normal humans coexist without exploitation or social conflict? Would the problem eventually be solved by the technology becoming affordable by all? Perhaps, though as with ordinary computers, effective use requires not only access but also training, and education systems must also deal with inequalities based on socioeconomic background.

*Computers can already beat the best human chess players. Will robots beat humans at soccer someday? Here robot players compete in the 2004 RoboCup tournament in Lisbon, Portugal.* (Photo ©RoboCup Federation)

Today Warwick continues as professor of cybernetics at the University of Reading. In addition to supervising robotics research programs, he is director of a program that obtains funding for university research in cooperation with technology companies.

Warwick's greatest continuing impact, though, is in his lectures and exploration of the promises and perils of cyborg technology. As Warwick said near the conclusion of *I, Cyborg:*

*The big question now faced by humanity is how we deal with the possibility of [being] superhumans? . . . Should we try to stop it, something which I feel, in practical terms, is not possible? Should we simply go for it, perhaps allowing commercial concerns to drive things forward, and profit through new needs and desires? Or should developments be policed or marshaled by governments through international collaborative agreements?*

The chances are good that these issues will increasingly enter into our social and political consciousness in the coming years.

# Chronology

| | |
|---|---|
| **1954** | Kevin Warwick born February 9 in Coventry, England |
| **1960s** | Kevin's father's operation sparks an interest in neurology and the brain |
| **1970s** | Warwick works as a telephone technician |
| **1974** | The TV series *The Six Million Dollar Man* popularizes the idea of bionic organisms for cyborgs |
| **1976** | Warwick enrolls in the University at Aston |
| **1979** | Warwick obtains his bachelor's degree in electrical and electronic engineering |
| **1982** | Warwick receives his Ph.D. at Imperial College, London |
| **1983–85** | Warwick becomes a lecturer at the University of Newcastle and receives an Oxford fellowship |
| **1988** | Warwick becomes professor of cybernetics at the University of Reading |
| **1990s** | Warwick and other researchers work on assistive technologies for the disabled |
| **1991** | Warwick begins work on the "Seven Dwarfs" cooperative learning robots |
| **1998** | Warwick receives a radio transponder implant in August; it communicates with computers and controls building doors and lights |
| **2002** | A neural array is implanted in Warwick's arm on March 14; experiments subsequently demonstrate the ability to send and receive nerve signals and control computers and robots |

# Further Reading

## Books

Warwick, Kevin. *I, Cyborg*. Chicago: University of Illinois Press, 2002.
> Autobiographical account with a focus on Warwick's implant experiments.

———. *March of the Machines: The Breakthrough in Artificial Intelligence*. Chicago: University of Illinois Press, 1997.
> Warwick surveys developments in artificial intelligence and robotics (including his own work at the University of Reading) and argues that a new age of intelligent machines will radically challenge many of our assumptions about intelligence.

## Articles

Sanchez-Klein, Jana. "Cyberfuturist Plants Chip in Arm to Test Human-Computer Interaction." CNN.com (from PC World.com), August 28, 1998. Available online. URL: http://www.cnn.com/TECH/computing/9808/28/armchip.idg/index.html. Accessed on September 2, 2005.
> Describes Warwick's experiment in which he implanted a silicon chip transponder in his arm, allowing him to communicate with computers without the use of a keyboard or other input device.

Warwick, Kevin. "I Want to Be a Cyborg." Comment letter to the *Guardian,* January 26, 2000. Available online. URL: http://www.guardian.co.uk/Archive/Article/0,4273,3954989,00.html.
> Warwick explains why he is willing to take the risks involved in extending human capabilities.

## Web Site

Professor Kevin Warwick. URL: http://www.kevinwarwick.com. Accessed on September 20, 2005.
> Warwick's home page at the University of Reading, including discussion of his human cyborg (implant) projects.

# CHRONOLOGY

| | |
|---|---|
| **1921** | The play *Rossum's Universal Robots* by Karel Capek adapts a Czech word meaning serf, or "forced laborer," to describe machines that can perform complex tasks |
| **1940s** | World War II spurs developments in computers, communication, and control devices |
| **1942** | Science fiction writer Isaac Asimov coins the term *robotics* and devises his "Three Laws" governing robot behavior |
| **1944** | Norbert Wiener calls for interdisciplinary conferences and research linking computing, control engineering, and biological sciences |
| **1948** | Norbert Wiener publishes *Cybernetics,* a comprehensive analysis of communication and control in machines and living things |
| **1950** | Grey Walter's robotic "tortoises" demonstrate how simple interactions can lead to complex behavior |
| **1956** | Joseph Engelberger and George Devol found Unimation and begin development of the first industrial robot |
| **1961** | The first Unimate robot begins work at a General Motors automobile factory |
| **1963** | The computer-controlled Rancho Arm demonstrates the utility of robots for helping handicapped persons |
| **1970** | SRI International's Shakey is the first robot to navigate autonomously using artificial intelligence |
| **1979** | The Stanford Cart, further developed by Hans Moravec, uses cameras and a computer to thread its way through a room filled with chairs |

| | |
|---|---|
| **1982** | Marc Raibert creates the first robot that can hop and keep its balance |
| **1984** | Joseph Engelberger founds HelpMate Robotics to develop service robots |
| **1986** | Marc Raibert establishes the Leg Laboratory at MIT and demonstrates bipedal robot acrobats |
| **Early 1990s** | Rodney Brooks develops Cog, a robot with humanlike ways of "paying attention" |
| | Cynthia Breazeal extends the principles behind Cog to create Kismet, a "sociable" robot modeled after a human infant |
| **1997** | NASA's six-wheeled *Sojourner* robot explores Mars |
| **1998** | Hans Moravec predicts that robots will achieve human intelligence by 2040 |
| | Kevin Warwick uses a radio chip in his arm to communicate with and customize his computerized environment |
| **2000** | Honda unveils Asimo, an agile humanoid robot that can walk, run, and even dance |
| | Colin Angle, Helen Greiner, and Rodney Brooks of iRobot market a robot doll called "My Real Baby" |
| **2002** | iRobots Roomba robot vacuum cleaner is introduced |
| | Kevin Warwick demonstrates two-way connection between the human nervous system and a robot |
| **2004** | U.S. Defense Department finances the development of robotic dogs to carry supplies for soldiers |
| **2005** | iRobot introduces new versions of "packbot" military robot |
| | A robot-controlled Volkswagen Touareg SUV designed by Stanford University wins a 132-mile race through the Nevada desert |

# GLOSSARY

**algorithm**   a set of specified steps that enable a computer or robot to accomplish a particular task

**analog**   continuously variable (as in the motion of the human body) rather than moving in discrete steps, as in digital computation, stepper motor motion, and so on. *See also* DIGITAL

**android**   a robot that has generally human features (such as a movable head and grasping arms) and that can see and respond to the environment in humanlike ways. *See also* CYBORG

**anthropomorphism**   the tendency of people to treat animals or robots as though they were persons. Humanlike robots often evoke such responses

**articulated geometry**   the development of robotic arms or legs that involve segments connected by joints, allowing versatility of motion

**artificial intelligence (AI)**   the attempt to get computers or robots to behave in ways that resemble human intelligence. Examples include vision and image recognition, learning, problem-solving techniques, and the ability to understand natural language

**artificial life (AL)**   the effort to simulate living organisms or ecologies using computer software or robots. Features can include behaviors (feeding, mating, and so on) as well as genetic inheritance and evolution

**Asimo (Advanced Step in Mobility)**   a humanoid demonstration robot manufactured by Honda Corporation in Japan

**Asimov's laws**   conceived by science fiction writer Isaac Asimov, the three laws were to be built into the structure of a robot's brain. They would require that robots prevent harm to humans, obey humans, and protect themselves—in that order

**automated guided vehicle** a robot cart or truck that operates by itself but follows rails or a guide wire and has only limited navigational capabilities

**automaton** a mechanism that can automatically perform a series of actions under the control of cams, gears, and other devices. Unlike a true robot, an automaton does not change its behavior in response to the environment

**autonomous robot** a robot that contains its own computer system, is mobile, and carries out its functions without direct human supervision

**behavior** in robots, the determination of actions based upon sensor data from the environment or internal states maintained in the robot's memory. Simple behaviors are equivalent to reflexes in living things, while complex behaviors can emerge from the interaction of many programs

**bipedal robot** a robot that walks on two legs like a human

**bot** popular colloquial term for "robot"

**Cog** robot built by Rodney Brooks at MIT in the early 1990s. Consisting only of a torso and head, the robot interacts mainly through eye movement, facial expressions, and vocalizations

**cognitive science** the study of information processing or thought in humans, machines, or animals. It is an interdisciplinary field that draws upon computer science, neurology, psychology, and other fields

**collision avoidance** systems designed to prevent a robot from bumping into obstacles such as furniture, rocks, or people. When a visual or sonar sensor detects a nearby object, robots of varying degrees of sophistication may go into reverse, turn, or plot a precise course around the object

**cybernetics** term coined by mathematician Norbert Wiener for the science of machine control and regulation; from a Greek word meaning "steersman" or "governor"

**cyborg** a "cybernetic organism" consisting of both artificial and biological components. In a sense, a person with a computer-controlled artificial arm would be a sort of cyborg. *See also* ANDROID

**degrees of freedom** the number of different ways in which something (such as a robot arm) can move. Robot arms normally have at least three degrees of freedom; human arms have seven (because of the separate pivots at the shoulder and elbow)

**digital** coming in discrete "chunks" that can be represented by numbers, as in a modern computer. *See also* ANALOG

**digitization** the process of turning incoming information into "chunks" having specific numerical values, as with pixels in a digital photograph.

**distributed system** an architecture where processing is carried out by many separate cooperating units rather than being controlled centrally

**dynamic walking** walking in which the center of balance is adjusted by exerting opposing forces—in a sense, controlled falling. This is how people walk; the first walking robots maintained a static balance and moved only one or two legs at a time

**edge detection** the ability of a robot or computer vision system to determine the boundaries of objects and thus their shape and nature. For example, a robot truck would need to be able to locate a road's edges and lane markings

**effector** something in a robot that manipulates the environment, such as by closing a hand. Roughly analogous to a muscle. A manipulator (hand) on the end of a robot arm is called an end effector

**embodied robot** Rodney Brooks's term for a robot that is capable of perceiving and reacting to the world through its body, as does an animal

**exoskeleton** a powered framework of joints, segments, and effectors that can be controlled by the user using normal muscle movements (and, in the latest developments, nerve impulses). The exoskeleton can thus serve as an artificial limb for a disabled person or for working with hazardous materials. An exoskeleton can also be a powered framework that can be attached to the body and used to increase strength, add to carrying capacity, or provide protection

**extropianism** (also called transhumanism) a philosophical movement that advocates the transformation of humanity through advanced technologies such as robotics, genetics, and nanotechnology. Its goal is to transcend existing physical limitations, explore human potential, and perhaps achieve immortality

**feedback**   the adjustment of a mechanism (such as a thermostat) in response to changes in its environment. *See also* CYBERNETICS

**fovea**   a thickening of nerves near the center of the eye, enabling much higher image resolution than is available at the periphery

**futurist**   a researcher or writer who tries to identify possible future developments or trends. For example, some futurists believe that robots with human-level intelligence may arrive by the middle of the 21st century

**gait**   the way in which the legs of an animal or robot move during locomotion

**hobby robot**   (also called educational robot) a robot, usually part of a kit, designed for demonstrating principles of robotics or experimentation by students or hobbyists. An example is the popular Lego Mindstorms

**industrial robot**   a robot used in a factory to move materials or perform repetitive tasks such as assembly or painting. The robot moves on a fixed track and has only limited ability to adapt to changes in its environment

**insect robot**   a legged robot that mimics the relatively simple, distributed nervous system of an insect. *See also* ROBOT SWARM

**Kismet**   a robot created by Cynthia Breazeal to emulate the behaviors, learning processes, and emotions of an infant

**lander**   a space probe that can land on the surface of a planet but does not have independent movement capability. *See also* ROVER

**mapping**   in robotics, the process by which a robot combines and analyzes sensor data in order to build a representation of the world, including the shapes and locations of objects

**MIP**   a million instructions per second; a basic measure of computer processing power. By the late 1990s computers were reaching 1,000 MIPS, or a billion instructions per second

**mobile robot**   a robot capable of moving freely. It is usually equipped with systems for navigating around the environment

**Moore's Law**   the observation that computer power roughly doubles every 18 months to two years. This has held true since the 1940s and has led some futurists to predict robots with human-like intelligence will arrive around 2040

**nanotechnology**   building on a molecular or atomic scale. Such machines could include tiny self-replicating robots or vastly more powerful components for conventional robots and computers

**navigation system**   the facility in a mobile robot responsible for determining destinations and plotting safe paths to them

**neural implant**   an electronic device (such as a small chip with electrodes) that is directly connected to the nervous system. It can detect and relay nerve signals as well as introduce outside signals into the nervous system

**neural network**   a large array of processing nodes that can be "trained" to perform a task by reinforcing those that are successful. Applications include facial recognition and image processing

**occupancy grid**   a navigation method where surrounding space is divided into numerous three-dimensional cells and sensor data are analyzed to determine a probability that a given cell is occupied by something. Paths can then be plotted to avoid possible obstructions

**odometery**   a relatively primitive form of navigation where a robot's position is updated by recording direction and displacement (distance traveled)

**prosthesis**   an artificial limb intended to replace a lost leg or arm and to replicate as much of its natural function as possible. Advanced prostheses use much of the same technology as robot arms, along with sophisticated muscular or possibly neural connections to the body

**RFID**   (radio frequency identification) an embetted chip that broadcasts identifying information in response to a radio signal

**robot**   a machine that is capable of carrying out complex tasks and responding to its environment. From a Czech word meaning serf, or "forced laborer"

**robotics**   the discipline concerned with the design and operation of robots. It is actually an interdisciplinary pursuit drawing from computer science, electronic and mechanical engineering, and even biology

**robot swarm**   a group of relatively small and simple robots that can cooperate to carry out tasks such as finding mines

**rover**   a mobile robot that can explore hard-to-reach areas such as the surface of other planets. The robot receives remote commands but has some autonomous functions

**saccade**   a rapid movement of the eyes to lock onto an object of interest

**sensor**   anything that gathers data from the environment, such as a camera or a sonar. In biology, sensors are often called receptors

**service robot** a mobile robot designed for nonindustrial workplaces for tasks such as delivering supplies

**Shakey** an early mobile robot at Stanford University in the early 1960s. It was named for its rather precarious camera attachments

**situated robot** Rodney Brooks's term for a robot that responds directly to sensory input in a way similar to reflexes in animals

**sociable robot** term coined by researcher Cynthia Breazeal for a robot that can appropriately understand and react to vocal intonation, facial expressions, body language, and other cues

*Sojourner* the first mobile Mars rover, which was the fruit of many years of mobile robotics research. Named for the American abolitionist Sojourner Truth, the rover landed on Mars in July 1997

**space probe** a robotic, pilotless spacecraft that is controlled by instructions from controllers on Earth

**Stanford Cart** a wheeled platform for mobile robot experiments used at the Stanford Artificial Intelligence Laboratory mainly in the 1970s

**subsumption architecture** a form of robot design in which many separate components interact to create complex behaviors. More complex behaviors such as exploration and mapping are layered on top of simpler behaviors such as locomotion and collision avoidance

**teleology** consideration of organisms or devices in terms of their ultimate purpose or goal. *See also* CYBERNETICS

**vision system** the components such as cameras, image processors, and software that a robot uses to detect and characterize objects in its environment

**zero momentum point (ZMP)** the point on a walking robot where the angular momentum (resulting from gravity and other accelerations acting on the robot) is zero. A dynamic walking robot can remain stable as long as the ZMP is within the area of support of the feet

# FURTHER RESOURCES

## Books

Aylett, Ruth. *Robots: Bringing Intelligent Machines to Life?* Hauppage, N.Y.: Barron's Educational, 2002.

> A well-illustrated guide to the functional problems and innovations in modern robotics.

Foerst, Anne. *God in the Machine: What Robots Teach Us about Humanity and God.* New York: Dutton, 2004.

> The author, a theologian and artificial intelligence researcher, uses a new generation of robots (such as Cog and Kismet) to ask fundamental questions about the meaning and purpose of humanity.

Freedman, David H. *Brainmakers: How Scientists Are Moving beyond Computers to Create a Rival to the Human Brain.* New York: Touchstone, 1994.

> Describes a number of interesting approaches to designing intelligent behavior in robots.

Garreau, Joel. *Radical Evolution: The Promise and Peril of Enhancing Our Minds, Our Bodies—and What It Means to Be Human.* New York: Doubleday, 2004.

> The author includes robotics in a set of technologies (also including genetic engineering, information processing, and nanotechnology) that offer the possibility to transform human nature.

Gibilisco, Stan, ed. *The McGraw-Hill Illustrated Encyclopedia of Robotics & Artificial Intelligence.* New York: McGraw-Hill, 1994.

> Includes A-to-Z entries for concepts, technologies, and brief biographies.

Ichbiah, Daniel. *Robots: From Science Fiction to Technological Revolution.* New York: Henry Abrams, 2005.

> A copiously illustrated "visual survey" of robots in practical applications and in popular culture.

Jones, David. *Mighty Robots: Mechanical Marvels That Fascinate and Frighten.* Toronto: Annick Press, 2005.

**175**

A fascinating overview of the development of robotics and the many uses of robots today, including exploration, factory work, medicine, toys, and entertainment. For young adult readers.

Menzel, Peter, and Faith D'Aluisio. *Robo Sapiens: Evolution of a New Species.* Cambridge, Mass.: MIT Press, 2000.

A lavishly illustrated gallery of innovative robots and interviews with their creators.

Moravec, Hans. *Robot: Mere Machine to Transcendent Mind.* New York: Oxford University Press, 1999.

A prominent robotics researcher describes the developments in modern robotics that point to a future in which robots overtake humans in intelligence.

Thro, Ellen. *Robotics: Intelligent Machines for the New Century.* New Edition. New York: Facts On File, 2003.

Describes the history and concepts behind robotics, including anatomy, functions, intelligence, and applications.

Warwick, Kevin. *March of the Machines: The Breakthrough in Artificial Intelligence.* Chicago: University of Illinois Press, 1997.

Warwick suggests that robotics and artificial intelligence have already accomplished far more than most people realize. More breakthroughs are coming, and people need to find creative ways to respond.

Wood, Gaby. *Edison's Eve: A Magical History of the Quest for Mechanical Life.* New York: Knopf, 2002.

Describes the development of clever, intricate automatons through the centuries, as well as the literature and folklore that celebrated them.

## Internet Resources

A Brief History of Robotics. MSNBC. Available online. URL: http://www.msnbc.com/modules/robot_history. Accessed on August 1, 2005.

A slide-show view of the development of robots, with emphasis on robots in popular culture and in a variety of applications.

Lego Mindstorms. Available online. URL: http://mindstorms.lego.com/eng/default.asp?domainredir=www.legomindstorms.com. Accessed on September 25, 2005.

Presents products and activities based on the popular LEGO-based robotics kits.

Mars Exploration Rover Mission. Available online. URL: http://marsrovers.jpl.nasa.gov/gallery/images.html. Accessed on August 5, 2005.

This Jet Propulsion Laboratory site contains news, activities, archives, and multimedia files relating to NASA's Mars rovers.

RoboCup. Available online. URL: http://www.robocup.org. Accessed on September 15, 2005.
> Site of a project to promote robotics research using soccer as a test bed for many mobile robot skills. Conducts annual contests and aims to build a world championship soccer team of autonomous robots by 2050.

"Robot." Biography.ms. Available online. URL: http://robot.biography.ms. Accessed on September 26, 2005.
> Extensive overview of the concepts and history of robotics, with links to related articles and sites.

Robotic Life. MIT Media Lab. Available online. URL: http://robotic.media.mit.edu. Accessed on August 5, 2005.
> Site of a project to develop cooperative robots that communicate in a variety of ways with one another and with humans.

Robotics in Japan. URL: http://transit-port.net/Lists/Robotics.Org.in.Japan.html. Accessed on September 15, 2005.
> Provides links to robotics organizations and projects in Japan; also has links to similar lists for Germany and Australia.

Robotics Links. URL: http://www.rdrop.com/~cary/html/robot_links.html. Accessed on September 15, 2005.
> Personal site of David Cary, with many links to robots by type and function, descriptions of robot components, news articles, and specific robots, organizations, and projects.

Robots Alive! Guide & Resources. Available online. URL: http://www.pbs.org/safarchive/4_class/45_pguides/pguide_705/4575_idx.html. Accessed on August 5, 2005.
> Teachers' guide for a *Scientific American Frontiers* television show about robotics. Includes some very interesting video downloads showing robots driving, walking, and interacting with people.

## Periodicals

### IEEE Transactions on Robotics
Published by the Institute for Electrical and Electronics Engineers
Online edition at URL: http://ieeexplore.ieee.org/sesrvlet/opac?punumber-8860
> The number one cited academic journal in robotics

### Personal Robotics News
(Online newsletter)
URL: http://www3.sympatico.ca/donroy/aboutprn.html
> Primarily for home robot builders and enthusiasts

### Robotics Trends
(Online newsletter)
URL: http://www.roboticstrends.com/PersonalRobotics+main.html
   Has news and features on personal robots, service robots, security and defense robots, and entertainment robots

### Servo Magazine
Published by T&L Publications Inc.
URL: http://www.servomagazine.com
P.O. Box 15277
North Hollywood, CA 91615-5277
Telephone: (877) 525-2539
   Magazine for amateur robotics enthusiasts; includes projects and feature articles about cutting-edge robotics

## Societies and Organizations

American Society for Cybernetics (http://www.asc-cybernetics.org) 2115 G Street NW, Suite 403, Washington, DC 20052 Telephone: (202) 994-1681.

Association for Computing Machinery (www.acm.org) One Astor Plaza, 1515 Broadway, 17th Floor, New York, NY 10036-5701 Telephone: (212) 869-7440

Carnegie-Mellon Robotics Institute. (http://www.ri.cmu.edu/) 5000 Forbes Avenue, Pittsburgh, PA 15213-3890 Telephone: (412) 268-3818

Computer Science and Artificial Intelligence Laboratory at the Massachusetts Institute of Technology. (www.csail.mit.edu) The Stata Center, Building 32, 32 Vassar Street, Cambridge, MA 02139 Telephone: (617) 253-5851

Institute for Electrical and Electronic Engineering Robotics and Automation Society. (http://www.ncsu.edu/IEEE-RAS/) 445 Hoes Lane, Piscataway, NJ 08855 Telephone: (800) 678-IEEE

MIT (Massachusetts Institute of Technology) Media Lab (www.media.mit.edu) Building E15, 77 Massachusetts Avenue, Cambridge, MA 02139-4307 Telephone: (617) 253-5960

Robotics Industry Association (www.roboticsonline.com) 900 Victors Way, Suite 140, P.O. Box 3724, Ann Arbor, MI 48106 Telephone: (734) 994-6088

Stanford Artificial Intelligence Laboratory (http://ai.stanford.edu/) Gates Building 1A, 353 Serra Mall, Stanford, CA 94305-9010 Telephone: (650) 723-9689

# INDEX